JOURNEY THROUGH DESPAIR

1880–1914

Journey

Through

Despair

1880-1914

TRANSFORMATIONS IN BRITISH
LITERARY CULTURE

by John A. Lester, Jr.

PRINCETON, NEW JERSEY
PRINCETON UNIVERSITY PRESS
1968

for Wendy

Acknowledgments

The theme of the following book has grown and become defined and crystallized over several years. Insofar as the crystal has now achieved edge and clarity, I owe much to the help given me along the way by colleagues who encouraged and advised and by friends who read with sympathetic care several early versions of the text. For the confirmations, corrections, and provocation which their friendship and wisdom have afforded me, I am indebted especially to Professors Walter E. Houghton and E.D.H. Johnson. Students at Haverford College; scholars of the faculty of Haverford and elsewhere; patient, meticulous seekers on the staffs of libraries in the United States and abroad—especially the staff of the British Museum—time and again all of these have given me perspective and have served as catalysts, and as guards against wishful thinking. To all of these, with no attribution of guilt-by-association where the final text may falter, I am deeply grateful. Alison Lester has devoted long hours to checking and confirming the references; Faith Kaltenbach to rendering a rough-hewn final manuscript into a workable final draft; and Mrs. Earl Sugg to the preparation of the present text in its typed form; and Janet Rubright has been invaluable in preparing the index.

In an early version, Chapter 7 ("Ecstasy") appeared in *English Literature in Transition* (VI, 4, 1963); I am grateful to the editors of that journal for their permission to present those materials in a revised form here.

Haverford College has been constantly considerate in its support of research for this study, particularly through

ACKNOWLEDGMENTS

its Faculty Research Fund, which made possible the purchase of otherwise inaccessible books and materials in photostat and microfilm.

My deepest debt I owe to my wife, who, as I have pursued a theme which at times appeared evanescent and will-o'-the-wispish, has borne with me selflessly in times of isolation, and when the "gemlike flame" burned low.

JOHN A. LESTER, JR.

Haverford College
April 1968

Contents

JOURNEY THROUGH DESPAIR

1880–1914

. . . la vie humaine commence de l'autre côté du désespoir.

Jean-Paul Sartre (*Les Mouches,* III, ii)

Introduction

The terrain of English literary culture from the death of
Thomas Carlyle to the First World War is still difficult
for us to see in clear perspective. Some contours are hazy
simply because we do not know enough. Manuscripts,
letters, the records of the passing moods and motives of
the turn of the century, all of which help to focus and
clarify our vision of an age, are not yet fully available to
us. We see a scene crossed by conflicting schools and
trends, impassioned crusades that flare up and fail; we see
it as an age of intensity, lust for life, and despair; and as
one of clique, club, and coterie. It seems, paradoxically,
an age charged with a vibrant energy matched only by its
world-weariness, a utopian resolve matched only by its
despair. Paradox, to be sure, is a lively thing; it provokes
by revealing the present limitations of what we know, and
it challenges us to seek a fuller vision of what lies beyond.
Recent criticism has shown the increasing urgency of our
need to know more clearly this time of the *fin de siècle*.
The age itself had a passion for paradox, Whistlerian,
Wildean, Chestertonian—a passion which haunts our intelligence and impels us to discover what cultural unity or
impulse may have lurked behind those paradoxes in a
period which lies so close in the background of our own.
Was that period indeed "an end"? Or was it "a beginning"? Or, as we were told not long ago of the poets of
that age, was it simply exotic, "outside the main English
tradition"?[1]

[1] Frank Kermode, *Romantic Image* (New York: Chilmark
Press, 1961), p. 12. See also Helmut E. Gerber, "The Nineties:
Beginning, End, or Transition?" in *Edwardians and Late Vic-*

To have such fundamental questions so long unresolved becomes more worrisome if one suspects, as I do, that beneath the diversity of these years there was a major transformation taking place in man's imaginative orientation to the world. It is tantalizing to find in the literature of the turn of the century, which so often seems dated and strangely old, sudden moments which seem strangely new. Mingled with the charms of the period piece, there are sudden glimpses and forebodings of our own "modern" predicament. There are moods and aspirations in the period from 1880 to 1914 which our own culture has not willingly let die; there are prime movers of our own imaginative experience—Yeats, Joyce, Conrad, possibly D. H. Lawrence come first to mind—who were shaped in the crucible of that generation's tragedy. It is becoming not less but more difficult to rest with the riddles of the period, for their solution holds the intriguing promise of telling us more about ourselves.

The dates 1880 and 1914 are by no means sacrosanct in defining the period in question. What gives it its distinctive character is the clear emergence in English literary consciousness of a conviction that the known bearings of literary culture, whether humanist, romantic, or Victorian, have been forever lost. One can easily point to milestones marking the emergence of this conviction. Before the stated starting point of our period there were Darwin's *Origin of Species* (1859), Swinburne's *Poems and Ballads* (1866), the Franco-Prussian War (1870-1871), John Tyndall's Belfast Address to the British Association (1874), and the opening of the Grosvenor Gallery (1877)

---

torians, ed. Richard Ellmann (New York: Columbia, 1960), pp. 50-79.

to indicate the rapidly changing climate of thought, taste, and social ethos. Within the confines of our selected generation fall the founding of the Society for Psychical Research (1882), the darkling plain of Hardy's Wessex novels (1872-1896), the downfall of Oscar Wilde in 1895, the *Savoy*'s publication (1896), the Boer War (1899-1902), Victoria's death (1901), Haeckel's *Riddle of the Universe* (English translation, 1901), the first *Dreadnought* launched (1906), followed by the widening and deepening of the Kiel Canal, the outbreak of World War I in August 1914, and all over Europe the lights going out.

Through such an array of dates and signposts there is one trend to which the dates 1880 and 1914 give tangible and approximately accurate definition: the literary culture moved steadily from a suspicion (as it became manifest in Matthew Arnold) that the old bases of significant imaginative life were indefensible, to a widespread if not dominant conviction that they had altogether collapsed, as in Swinburne's

> We are not sure of sorrow,
> And joy was never sure;

as in Yeats's view of Lionel Johnson and Dowson exhibiting the "gravity of men who had found life out and were awakening from a dream"; as in Conrad's young sea-captain struck with "the creeping paralysis of a hopeless outlook."[2]

[2] Algernon Charles Swinburne, "The Garden of Proserpine" (1866), stanza 10; William Butler Yeats, "Anima Hominis," Sect. V in *Per Amica Silentia Lunae* (New York: Macmillan, 1918), p. 29; and Joseph Conrad, *The Shadow Line* (1915), Chap. 5 (New York: Doubleday, 1923), p. 93.

The general drift of these years has been detected before. Books like Edmund Wilson's *Axel's Castle* (1931), William York Tindall's *Forces in Modern British Literature* (1947), Frank Kermode's *Romantic Image* (1957), and Richard Ellmann and Charles Feidelson's critical anthology, *The Modern Tradition* (1965), all draw upon and speculate upon the premonitions of modernity in British literature of this period. The "Afterword on Bibliography" appended to the present study shows that richer and more detailed information has become available in recent years to illuminate the 1880-1914 period. Yet the *Geist* of the time, it has recently been remarked, "has continued to prove . . . singularly elusive."[3] It remains to us a generation of shifting, conflicting trends and motives. We still lack a coherent answer to the question that most of all needs an answer: What is the primary force which so unsettles, disperses, and disorients the imaginative experience of this period?

One might submit that the question needs no answer. If one believes that the imagination can live at peace with meaninglessness, with what an Indian *guru* once described to me as "the incoherent whim-wham of a freakful chaos," then it may be futile to seek for *causes* which make the life of the literary imagination more unsettled and uneasy in these years than in other generations. But if one starts, as I do, from another premise—if one accepts, as I do, Joan Bennett's comment illuminating Virginia Woolf: "Order and relation may or may not exist elsewhere, but

[3] Wendell V. Harris, "Identifying the Decadent Fiction of the Eighteen-Nineties," *English Fiction in Transition*, Vol. 5 (1962), p. 11.

they undoubtedly exist in the mind of man"[4]—then one must conclude that a world such as that which confronted this 1880-1914 generation, and which seemed to deprive man's being of all significance, must have had a deeply unsettling effect on its literary culture. And, since the unexamined life is not worth living, one is impelled to seek out the nature of the challenge posed by this despairing world-view, and to find how that challenge was met.

The literature itself gives convincing clues that, behind surface diversity, there was in fact a single underlying cultural crisis at work. Over and over again one is confronted with unexpected connections between motifs which had seemed totally disparate. William Ernest Henley, for example, we habitually read as a militant anti-aesthete; yet as early as 1893 Arthur Symons was finding close parallels between his work and Walter Pater's. One would hardly expect to hear Pater and Nietzsche spoken of in the same breath, yet Arthur Ransome devotes convincing pages to the striking affinity between them.[5] Motifs of social reform and of its seeming antithesis, aesthetic commitment, come together in the same author in this period, most manifestly in William Morris, as they had done in the work of his forebear, John Ruskin. Techniques of realism and im-

[4] Joan Bennett, *Virginia Woolf: Her Art as a Novelist*, 2nd edn. (Cambridge, Eng.: Cambridge University Press, 1964), p. 12.

[5] On Henley and Pater, see Symons, "The Decadent Movement in Literature," *Harper's New Monthly Magazine*, LXXXVII (November 1893), 866-867. The parallel is also touched upon in Jerome H. Buckley, *William Ernest Henley: A Study in the "Counter-Decadence" of the 'Nineties* (Princeton: Princeton University Press, 1945), p. 179. On Pater and Nietzsche, see Ransome, *Portraits and Speculations* (London: Macmillan, 1913), pp. 135-142.

pressionism separate and coalesce in the art and literature of the time. An author declares, "the aim of life is appreciation," and the spokesman is not Pater, not Wilde, not even Cunninghame Graham—but G. K. Chesterton! "The world is for me a collection of phenomena, which are to be studied and reproduced artistically," writes one seldom classed as an art-for-art's-saker, George Gissing.[6] These things, brief hints of kinship where none was expected, tease and tantalize. They gather to a conviction that there *was* a single crisis at work through this culture, and that there may be a synthesis which can be reached and described for this age of the willful, the petulant, the random, and the bizarre. The present book undertakes to suggest what sort of synthesis may be looked for, and where.

The invaluable critical biographies which have recently appeared cannot in themselves provide the basis of synthesis. Each man lives one life alone. Nor do I believe that social history and the tides of taste can provide the matrix for a unified view of the culture of the turn of the century. External accident plays too large a part here; and, in any case, to conclude that "lack of inhibition was the real besetting sin of the Naughty Nineties," or that a "spirit of mutual help" among artists turned to mutual hatred at the end of the century does not measurably ad-

[6] Chesterton, *Autobiography* (London: Hutchinson, 1937), p. 333; Gissing, letter to Algernon Gissing, July 18, 1883, quoted in Jacob Korg, *George Gissing: A Critical Biography* (Seattle: University of Washington Press, 1963), p. 71. The frequent interconnections of cultural trends in the late century have been commented on by Thomas Jay Garbaty, "The *Savoy*: 1896" (unpublished doctoral dissertation, University of Pennsylvania, 1957), pp. 110, 116, 130-131.

vance our understanding of the causes of cultural change.[7]
Even the disciplines of artistic criticism and theory, as
they disentangle the motives of formalism and aestheticism, and the curiously divergent passions of the *fin de
siècle* for hard, gemlike artistry on the one side and for
misty nocturnes on the other, even these do not appear to
me to bring into view the underlying cultural pattern of
the period.

This study takes its ground upon what may be called
man's imaginative conception of his place in the scheme
of things. It moves on the assumption that the rewards, the
aspirations, and the fundamental motives of human life—
and certainly of artistic achievement—are intimately dependent upon man's imaginative view of his condition.
Alfred North Whitehead maintains that "the mentality
of an epoch springs from the view of the world which is
. . . dominant in the educated sections of the communities
in question,"[8] but the student of literary culture can define the matter even more precisely. One can grant that
the conditions of man's physical well-being do directly
affect his sense of satisfaction and significance in life—
that the economic depressions, for example, and the rise
of the new Germany in the 1870s did contribute to the
groundnote of despair in England in the late century.
One can grant further that a deep satisfaction is achieved
in coming intellectually or metaphysically to terms with
the world, and that on these terms it was difficult to make

[7] The quotations are from Esmé Wingfield-Stratford, *Victorian
Sunset* (New York: William Morrow, 1932), p. 323, and William
Gaunt, *Aesthetic Adventure* (London: Jonathan Cape, 1945), pp.
121-124.

[8] Preface, *Science and the Modern World* (New York: Macmillan, 1931), p. ix.

sense out of the world as it was at the turn of the century. The world seen intellectually does certainly impinge on man's imagination and does much to modify it. Yet the artist is not a metaphysician. The artist's inspiration and rewards are something other than those of the intellect. He demands confidence in a world where his dreams and his craft can live, where what Edmund Burke once called the "great superstitions of the human heart" can be sustained. Circumstance, experience, and intellection can limit or shape the area of that confidence, but the imagination has its own resources as well, in the unseen worlds that yet might be, and in the intuitive knowledge of what is beautiful and redeeming in human experience. The imagination must in some fashion come to terms with what empirical and inductive experience describe as real, but beyond that it must build its own Byzantium, where the eternal is, and where beauty, symmetry, and ecstasy have their being. Colin Wilson makes the point dogmatically: "In every writer who possesses intensity of imagination, the imagination is closely bound up . . . with his notion of the meaning and purpose of human existence." Meaning and purpose may be hard to find, and the artist's imagination may at times be called on, as was George Gissing's, to "make a world within the world."[9]

My contention is that the years from 1880 to 1914 se-

[9] Wilson, *The Strength to Dream* (Boston: Houghton Mifflin, 1962), p. vii; Gissing, letter to Algernon Gissing, Sept. 22, 1835, in *Letters . . . to Members of His Family*, p. 169, quoted in Korg, *Gissing*, p. 92. Cf. Wilde's "little city of gold where the flute-player never wearies, and the spring never fades." Letter to R. H. Sherard, postmark May 17, 1883, in *The Letters of Oscar Wilde*, ed. Rupert Hart-Davis (London: Hart-Davis, 1962), p. 147.

verely jarred and shifted the bearings of man's imaginative life and left him at times bewildered as to how to recover his lost meaning and purpose. Such times are necessarily painful, and they carry overtones of tragedy. In literature it was a time of confusion and a nervous, often frenzied, search for new terms on which the imagination could live. This book is an attempt to describe the bewilderment and to define the critical challenge which confronted the imagination in this period, and to trace the most characteristic responses which that crisis provoked.

It should be clear, then, that this is not an exercise in literary criticism. It does not aim directly to distinguish major literary achievements of the period from minor ones, nor even the good from the bad. The thesis here advanced may well affect our critical estimates; it may shed light, for example, on the problem so often posed of late-century English literature: Why did it produce no classics? But other disciplines are illuminating, too. One of the hazards of exploring the imaginative condition of any epoch, and particularly of this epoch, is that it invites both support and attack from all areas of experience which do help to shape man's imaginative view of his place in the world. One delimitation of my study which I trust may engage such support, and may temper such attack, is that for the evidence and definition of the larger cultural crisis, I look specifically to *British literature* of the period. Within the limits of these materials I find the evidence of a single describable cultural crisis to be convincing. In seeking the influences which partly shaped the imaginative achievement of this literature, I have set no bounds other than trying to stay as close as possible to those forces which seem to have had the keenest impact on the imaginative life and self-image of the writers themselves in this generation.

My study is conceived in three phases: The Challenge posed to the literary imagination of this period; The Response in Three Modes to that challenge; and Applications, or three "test-cases," to demonstrate the value of the main thesis in interpreting distinctive themes and motives in the culture of the time. The drift toward disillusionment occupies us first, followed by an attempt to describe the nature of the underlying challenge. The responses considered are of the heart, the mind, and the imagination. There is something inspiriting in the responses that are made; "hope springs eternal." One is tempted to conclude that nothing, nothing "factual," nothing "realistic" —nothing nuclear—can defeat the human spirit. In any event, the prognoses of Gissing and Hardy that humanity would soon choose not to live have happily not been borne out in our time.

The three applications must speak and, if possible, convince for themselves. These draw directly on the literature of the period and view it in the light of the synthesis proposed. With these applications I must, as critic, mimic Joyce's artist and remain behind or beyond my handiwork, indifferent, paring my fingernails. It is on applications such as these that my case must rest; if such vistas into the literature of the time do indeed become clearer and more extensive, to that extent my main thesis has found validity.

One thing that did *not* afflict authors of this period was apathy. The terms of man's existence might be viewed, as they were by Thomas Hardy, as manifestly fixed—and manifestly intolerable; the implications of Darwin's work had finally closed the deterministic ring. Or the burden

might be felt as that of an incessantly changing, unknowable, and unpredictable existence. In either case the
plight induced no apathy, but rather the urgent and
pained necessity of a "transvaluation of all values,"[10] to
keep man's imaginative life alive under conditions which
seemed unlivable. It was to the generation of 1880-1914
that these crises were inescapably posed. More and more,
writers of this time had to find ways to dispense with
fixity and the absolutes, and to embrace uncertainty. It
was they who began to learn the lesson of our time, how
to live with uncertainty, how indeed to draw strength
and life from it. They left us few classics; but their reorientation, the beginnings of which are recorded in their
literature, exerts a greater shaping force on our own
imaginative life, I believe, than any we have known since
the Renaissance.[11]

[10] The quoted phrase is, of course, Friedrich Nietzsche's, proposed first in 1886 as a subtitle to his *The Will to Power* (published posthumously, 1901, 1906).

[11] I had thought that this idea was new with me until I met
Talcott Parsons' observation (*The Structure of Social Action*,
2nd edn. [Glencoe, Ill.: The Free Press, 1949], p. 5): "A revolution
of such magnitude . . . is hardly to be found occurring within the
short space of a generation, unless one goes back to about the
sixteenth century. What is to account for it?"

PART I: THE CHALLENGE

CHAPTER 1

Toward Disillusionment

No generation has been at peace with its time. Faced with terrors and impending chaos there have always been those who found it bliss to be alive, and ancient voices too, prophesying war. At the first dawn of the "Victorian" age Thomas Carlyle wrote that his generation had "walked by the light of conflagrations, and amid the sound of falling cities; and now there is darkness, and long watching till it be morning." But in the hubbub of the new London, Sam and Tony Weller were there too and found it "reasonably conwalessent" and "all wery capital." When the experience of an age can be assessed so variously, one must be careful in extracting common denominators.[1]

Yet the generation of the turn of the century was hypersensitive of its identity; it was inordinately fond of labeling itself. For this generation this was the "Age of Bovril," an age of newness of all kinds, the "yellow nineties," the "Beardsley period," the *fin de siècle*. In a phrase that crops up recurrently in literature of the time, "We are those upon whom the ends of the world are come."[2] Even in passing journalistic comment, one meets this consciousness that the age bore a special character and was

---

[1] Carlyle, "Characteristics" (1831), in *Critical and Miscellaneous Essays* (6 vols.; London, 1869), III, 363; and Charles Dickens, *Pickwick Papers* (1836-1837), Chaps. 37 and 33.

[2] Arthur Galton, "Assisi," *Century Guild Hobby Horse*, No. 3 (July 1886), p. 99. Cf. Walter Pater's description of *La Gioconda* in "Leonardo da Vinci," *The Renaissance* (1873). See I Cor. 10:11.

deeply sundered from generations gone before. Grant Allen likens Burne-Jones's painting to that of painters before Raphael, and yet it is unlike theirs too: it has the note of the nineteenth century in it, he says, "deep-questioning, mystic, uncertain, rudderless: faith gone; humanity left: heaven lost; earth realised as man's, the home and sole hope for the future."[3] The age was unanimously aware that it possessed an identity of its own; it is when we search for definitions of that identity that we find diversity and confusion.

At the risk of imposing arbitrary categories, we may best depict the cultural mood of these years as a drift from unrest to an intense excitement, from excitement to bewilderment, and thence to a darkening disillusionment. Obviously, no strict chronology will apply to these transitions. Different sensibilities respond to some stages more intensely than to others; the age at which a given author enters the literary scene very significantly affects, may even determine, his response. But the steady drift toward disillusionment seems to have left its mark inescapably on all the creative artists of the time.

⎰The causes of unrest lay partly in the facts of social history. New labor-saving machinery had been introduced, and prolonged agricultural and industrial depression in the 1870s and '80s had shaken again the stabilities of economic and class status. "Whole classes or strata of society . . . pushed their way out of the inarticulate and into the articulate part of the community[;] a kind of upstart arrogance became vocal with them."[4] New theories of social

[3] "The Celt in English Art," *Fortnightly Review*, XLIX, NS (February 1, 1891), 276.

[4] R.C.K. Ensor, *England 1870-1914* (Oxford: Oxford University

organization were advanced, and new socialist leagues were founded in the 1880s. By 1889 George Bernard Shaw could announce that it was statistically proven that England's civilization was "in an advanced state of rottenness." Robert Blatchford had come forth with an inspiration drawn from his youthful reading of tales of knight-errantry, and he did battle now on the social scene with the "fell dragons of privilege and prejudice."[5]

But the unrest had more than merely social causes. There was a new generation knocking at the door, and it demanded freedom from the old. It was an age of tension between father and son, an age of dreams and prophecies, an age of utopias.[6] Unrest pervaded man's material life, his thought, and his imagination. I have met with no sin-

---

Press, 1941), p. 304; see also Herman Ausubel, *The Late Victorians: A Short History* (New York: Van Nostrand, 1955), pp. 9-27.

[5] Shaw, "Economic [Basis of Socialism]," in *Fabian Essays*, G. Bernard Shaw, ed. (London, 1889), p. 24; and Blatchford, *My Eighty Years* (London: Cassell, 1931), p. 52.

[6] The classic records of filial dissension are Samuel Butler's *The Way of All Flesh* (1903) and Edmund Gosse, *Father and Son: A Study of Two Temperaments* (London, 1907). Professor Walter E. Houghton notes the increased intensity of father-son conflicts in years just preceding our period (*The Victorian Frame of Mind: 1830-1870* [New Haven: Yale University Press, 1957], pp. 81, 83-85). See also Wilde's *An Ideal Husband* (1895), Act II; Shaw's preface to Stephen Winsten, *Salt and His Circle* (London: Hutchinson, 1951), pp. 10-11; and Richard Ellmann, *Yeats: The Man and the Masks* (New York: Dutton, 1958), p. 21. Cf. Ivan Turgenev, *Fathers and Sons* (1862).

Of utopias and prophecies the most influential were Edward Bellamy's *Looking Backward* (1888), William Morris's *News from Nowhere* (1891), H. G. Wells' *A Modern Utopia* (1905), and W. H. Hudson's *A Crystal Age* (1906). See also Archibald Henderson, *George Bernard Shaw: Man of the Century* (New York: Appleton-Century-Crofts, 1956), p. 339.

gle study of man's spiritual condition in this period that does not openly recognize an instability which had entered into man's inner life. It may be called a "restlessness . . . in our veins," a "disquiet in the breasts of men," or "a consciousness of unrest and anxiety, . . . a vague feeling of alarm." The malaise touches the heart of every thinker and writer of the time.[7]

But one of the excitements of this culture is that, as in the Renaissance when a new philosophy, in John Donne's words, called "all in doubt," many early reactions at the turn of the century were not of frenzied despair, but of renewed vitality. Henry W. Nevinson gives the most concise record I have found of how such responses could come about: "For me, as for so many people in that variegated age of English life, [it was] a period of strangely vivid interests and strangely diverse pursuits. We were simultaneously, and almost equally, attracted by the soldier, enthusiastic for the rebel, clamorous for the poor, and devoted to the beautiful. Some of us were moved most by one of these incitements, some by another; but many, like myself, were moved by all four together, and we recognised no contradiction in the objects of our admiration or desire. The apparent contradictions were reconciled in a renewed passion—a glowing intensity—of life as we issued from the rather chilly rationalism and moralising of former years."[8] Intensity poured into all modes of

[7] The three quotations are from Lawrence Binyon, "On Certain Confusions of Modern Life . . . ," *Century Guild Hobby Horse*, No. 18 (April 1890), p. 59; Henry Drummond, *Natural Law in the Spiritual World* (London, 1889), p. xxi; and Laurence Oliphant, *Scientific Religion* . . . (London, 1888), p. 2.

[8] *Changes and Chances* (London: Nisbet 1923), p. 109; see also

6

life and thought and gave to each what seems in retrospect an energy and fervor in excess of its proper share.

London became, more than it had ever been before, the literary Mecca of this time in Britain; artists and authors all converged on London. They met with the hackwork of Grub Street at the start—it was the heyday of the new journalism; but each author brought a hope that his own flair, his own individual accent of style and personality, might make its mark on the vibrant age.[9] There was expectancy abroad that some new note would be struck in literature and the arts, something to catalyze and to express the strange new current mood. Each author newly arrived in London hoped that he might ride "on the crest of the wave that was sweeping away the Victorian tradition." This could be "one of the world's great mornings," moving at once "on to great things and [he] could help it move." "What uproar!" shouts Max Beerbohm. "Around me seethed swirls, eddies, torrents, violent cross-currents of human activity."[10] With such electric excitement in the air it is small wonder that the period's cultural pattern is hard to define, and small wonder that its literature is fraught with so many seemingly conflicting trends.

John Masefield, *So Long to Learn* (New York: Macmillan, 1952), p. 75.

[9] A brief discussion of the causes and character of the rise of late-century literary journalism is given in John A. Lester, Jr., *John Davidson: A Grub Street Bibliography* (Charlottesville: University of Virginia Press, 1958), pp. 3-5.

[10] The quotations are from Evelyn Sharp, *Unfinished Adventure* (London: John Lane, 1933), p. 56; Edgar Jepson, *Memories of a Victorian* (London: Gollancz, 1933), p. 238; and Max Beerbohm, "Diminuendo," in *Works and More* (London: John Lane, 1930), p. 135.

Many motives of the late century partook of this new excitement. The New Hedonism—detected and named by Grant Allen—was one, bringing with it the extraordinary rage for Fitzgerald's *Omar*.[11] Activism was another, transformed from Ulysses' will "to strive, to seek, to find, and not to yield" to a rejoicing in vigorous action, in the struggle itself—as in Kipling and Henley and in Stevenson's "brave gymnasium" of the world—rather than in striving toward a known end.[12] Professor J. H. Buckley has written well on this subject and has pointed out its forebears in Victorian literature: the pride of self-help in the captain of industry and the self-made man, Ulysses' quest, Carlyle's gospel of work.[13] Without question, the resort to action purely as an escape from doubt had been a literary motif earlier in the century; one recalls Tennyson's spokesman in "Locksley Hall": "I myself must mix

[11] Grant Allen, "The New Hedonism," *Fortnightly Review*, LV, NS (March 1, 1894), 377-392. Recall Oscar Wilde's hedonistic revision of Scripture: "Let us get what pleasure we may in the fleeting days; for the night cometh, and the silence that can never be broken." (Frank Harris, *Oscar Wilde: His Life and Confessions* [2 vols., New York: Frank Harris, 1916], II, 409.) On *Omar's* popularity, see Joseph McCabe, *Edward Clodd* (London: John Lane, 1932), p. 90; cf. A.J.A. Symons, *The Quest for Corvo* (London: Cassell, 1955), p. 134.

[12] The "brave gymnasium" phrase appears in Stevenson's "Dedication" to *Virginibus Puerisque and Other Papers* (1881). Cf. Morley Roberts' interpretation of Hudson's lesson as being "that the fight and not the victory remains man's reward" (*W. H. Hudson: A Portrait* [London: Nash and Grayson, 1924], p. 143); and W.E.H. Lecky's statement that more and more men were finding "in active, useful and unselfish work . . . the best refuge from the perplexities of belief. . . ." (*The Map of Life* [London, 1899], p. 213.)

[13] Jerome Hamilton Buckley, *William Ernest Henley* (Princeton: Princeton University Press, 1945), Chap. I.

with action, lest I wither by despair." But in the later century the motif is markedly more pervasive and intense, and more radical in its skepticism of the goal of action. In Carlyle and Tennyson there is often a tacit assumption that work lights the way toward truth—"'Do the Duty which lies nearest thee'.... The second duty will already have become clearer";[14] in the late century there is less confidence that a truth or a newly found moral obligation awaits. The activist's immersement is rather in the action for its own sake.

Intensity seems more and more a hallmark of this fin-de-siècle culture. It informs aestheticism—as in Pater's resolve to "be present always at the focus where the greatest number of forces unite in their purest energy."[15] It informs the heightened demand for tales of adventure and far-off lands, a demand met by the romances of Kipling, Hudson, Haggard, Stevenson, and of course Joseph Conrad, who became much provoked at his readers' insistence on taking him as a writer of sea stories. There is an extraordinary intensity in the imperialism and socialism of the turn of the century; both became charged with an overplus of fervor which exalted each at times almost to religion. To G. K. Chesterton, socialism and imperialism seemed "the two great movements" of his youth. Stewart Headlam found that it is now the "main function of the Christian church . . . to carry out the principles of Socialism"; John Davidson, in his late vein of oracular dogmatism, could state that "poetry is the will to live and the will to power; poetry is the empire." When

[14] Thomas Carlyle, Sartor Resartus, Bk. II, Chap. 9.
[15] "Conclusion," The Renaissance (1873). The "Conclusion" first appeared in 1868, as the conclusion of Walter Pater's review of poetry of William Morris.

Stephen Phillips wrote in 1899 of the lack in contemporary poetry of "some great compelling . . . purpose," he had to make one exception—"the wave of emotion and enthusiasm which has visited us lately . . . roused by the splendour and the fact of empire."[16]

Embracing all such excitements was the motive simply to live life to the fullest, "to live life significantly—keenly and beautifully, personally and, if need be, daringly; to win from it its fullest satisfactions . . . and most exhilarating experiences."[17] It is the self-reliance of Emerson and Whitman much heightened, intensified by influences of Max Stirner and Nietzsche, and by Villiers de l'Isle Adam: "Become the flower of thyself!" Oscar Wilde strikes the same note: "The aim of life is self-development. To realize one's nature perfectly—that is what each of us is here for."[18] To this theme the loud clamor in life and in fiction for the emancipation of women from the marital bond was closely related. If women were to achieve full self-development and self-realization, the societal contract which simply restricts and precommits must be

[16] Quotations from Chesterton, *Autobiography* (London: Hutchinson, 1937), p. 111; Headlam, *The Socialist's Church* (London, 1907), p. 48; Davidson, "The Poetry of Empire," *Outlook* (Feb. 4, 1905), p. 161; and Phillips, "A Field for Modern Verse," *Dome*, II (1899), p. 91. For other statements of socialism and imperialism as religions, see R. J. Campbell, *The New Theology* (London, 1907), Chaps. 1, 13-14, and J. A. Cramb, *Reflections on the Origins and Destiny of Imperial Britain* (London, 1900).

[17] Richard Le Gallienne, *The Romantic '90s* (London: Putnam, 1951), p. 157.

[18] *The Picture of Dorian Gray* (1891), Chap. 2. For earlier Victorian forebears of the theme, see Houghton, *Victorian Frame of Mind*, pp. 287-291; and John Stuart Mill: The Creator ". . . gave all human faculties that they might be cultivated and unfolded. . . ." (*On Liberty* [1859], Chap. 3.)

done away with; the heart—"which signs no documents"[19]
—must be free. The demand for women's freedom was
expressed in actuality in the Married Woman's Property
Acts of 1892 and 1893, and in fiction in Olive Schreiner's
The Story of an African Farm (1883), Grant Allen's
The Woman Who Did (1895), Hardy's *Jude the Obscure*
(1895), Forster's *The Longest Journey* (1907), and in
many novels of H. G. Wells and others.[20]

The intense drive toward life at its fullest pressed on
into moods of uncertainty, bewilderment, decadence. This
was not simply the Byronic exhaustion, where "the sword
wears out the sheath," nor the Swinburnean "too much
love of living" (though Dowson's poetry holds records of
such moments). It was a hunger for experience such as
that which prompted Wilde to announce that "sin is the
only real color-element left in modern life," or, even more
poignantly, to his pathetic resolve, "I must go as far as
possible. . . . Something must happen . . . something
else." It tempted Lionel Johnson to write that

> . . . all the things of beauty burn
> With flames of evil ecstasy.[21]

This is the response which mainly invokes the term
decadent, a response succinctly described by Le Gallienne
early in the 1890s: "To notice only the picturesque effect
of a beggar's rags, like Gautier; the colour-scheme of a

[19] E. M. Forster, "What I Believe," in *Two Cheers for Democracy* (New York: Harcourt, Brace, and World, 1951), p. 68.

[20] Houghton, *Victorian Frame of Mind*, pp. 361-364, gives evidence of early Victorian precedents for this motif.

[21] The quotations are from Oscar Wilde, *Dorian Gray*, Chap. 2; André Gide, *Oscar Wilde: In Memoriam* . . . trans. Bernard Frechtman (New York: Philosophical Library, 1949), p. 17; and Johnson, "The Dark Angel" (1893).

tipster's nose, like Mr. Huysmans; to consider one's mother merely prismatically, like Mr. Whistler—these are examples of the decadent attitude." The best description of all is still Arthur Symons': "[Late-century decadence] has all the qualities that mark the end of great periods, the qualities that we find in the Greek, the Latin, decadence: an intense self-consciousness, a restless curiosity in research, an over-subtilizing refinement upon refinement, a spiritual and moral perversity. . . . To fix the last fine shade, the quintessence of things; to fix it fleetingly; to be a disembodied voice, and yet the voice of the human soul: that is the ideal of Decadence."[22]

From intensity, relentlessly to disillusionment and despair—perhaps the result was inevitable. How can one insist on further and further extremes of experience without being pressed to the *outré* and the bizarre, and to the

[22] The quotations are from Le Gallienne, "Considerations Suggested by Mr. Churton Collins' 'Illustrations of Tennyson,'" *Hobby Horse*, No. 27 (July 1892), p. 81; and Symons, "The Decadent Movement in Literature," *Harper's New Monthly Magazine*, LXXXVII (November 1893), 858-859, 862. Lionel Johnson's diagnosis ("A Note upon the Practice and Theory of Verse at the Present Time Obtaining in France," *Hobby Horse*, No. 22 [April 1891], 61-66), is in substantial agreement.

Students of the phenomenon of decadence should consider, in addition to the two preceding references to Symons and Le Gallienne: Max Nordau, *Degeneration* (1895); Holbrook Jackson, *The Eighteen-Nineties* (1913), Chap. 3; Donald Davidson, "Introduction," *British Poetry of the Eighteen-Nineties* (New York: Doubleday, Doran, 1937); Buckley's *Henley*; C.E.M. Joad, *Decadence: A Philosophical Inquiry* (London: Faber and Faber, 1948); Clyde de L. Ryals, "Toward a Definition of *Decadent* as Applied to British Literature of the Nineteenth Century," *JAAC*, XVII, 1 (Sept. 1958), 85-92; Robert L. Peters, "Toward an 'Undefinition' of Decadent as Applied to British Literature of the Nineteenth Century," *JAAC*, XVIII, 1 (Sept. 1959), 258-264.

one step beyond what the human sensibility can bear? Wilde was compelled so: "We must always want the most tragic." The same fatal *élan* may be hidden in Yeats' conclusion: "We begin to live when we have conceived life as tragedy."[23] The very knowledge that a century was ending seems to have contributed to the mood; and coupled with the urge toward maximal experience and beyond, there grew the widespread notion that mankind had lost vitality at the *fin de siècle*, had become hypersensitive, effete, run down, "ending in decrepitude."[24] The notion runs through English and European literature of the period with startling persistence: "We are all of us just nothing but 'Epigoni'!"; "*les derniers fils d'une race épuisée*"; and

> Curs'd from the cradle and awry they come,
>   Masking their torment from a world at ease;
> On eyes of dark entreaty, vague and dumb,
>   They bear the stigma of their souls' disease.[25]

The mood shapes characters as diverse as Huysmans' Des Esseintes, Mann's child Hanno, and Hardy's Father Time.

[23] Gide, *Oscar Wilde*, p. 15; and Yeats, *The Trembling of the Veil* (1922), Bk. I, Sect. 21, in *The Autobiography of William Butler Yeats* (Garden City, New York: Doubleday, 1958), p. 128.

[24] George Moore, "The Future Phenomenon (*From the French of Stephane Mallarmé*)," *Savoy*, No. 3 (July 1896), p. 98.

[25] The Epigoni quotations are from Albert Schweitzer, *Out of My Life and Thought* (trans. C. T. Campion, New York: Holt, Rinehart and Winston, 1949), p. 146; D. H. Lawrence, *Sons and Lovers* (1913), Chap. 7 (New York: Viking, 1958), p. 149; and Edmund Gosse, "Neurasthenia" (1894). Cf. Friedrich Nietzsche's view of modern man as suffering from "an impoverished life and hereditary exhaustion" ("The Four Great Errors," Sect. 2, in *The Twilight of the Idols* [English translation by Thomas Common, 1899]).

Still another impulse toward disillusionment came from the realistic bent of much of the literature of this time. It is a further paradox of this culture that the intensity which led some to romantic adventure and escape from urban drabness led others to focus on the actualities of contemporary city life, and to reveal remorselessly its sordidness. Thus we find one author telling us, "The will to romance: that, in a phrase, was the motive philosophy of the '90s," while another will state of the same decade, "We are wholly given up to realism. . . . Little by little, even our children are losing this happy gift of believing the incredible."[26]

Granted, the realist was able to find romance in the realism of London streets as well. Urban realism discovered beauty in London's Thames and East End and in its mud and poverty that had not been found there before. But the groundnote of late-century realism was heavy and sorrowing, recording London as a city heaving and festering, aching and spiritless, where men "grow sickly, like grass under a stone."[27] Settings that once had been an evocative setting for romantic action became sordid and dehumanizing: "He would have preferred a more congenial spot, but, as usually happens, in place of a romantic field or solemn aisle for his tale, it was told while they walked up and down over a floor littered with rotten cabbage-leaves, and amid all the usual squalors of decayed

[26] Le Gallienne, *Romantic '90s*, p. 157; and Edmund Gosse, *Gossip in a Library* (London, 1891), pp. 325, 329.

[27] W. R. Lethaby, "Of Beautiful Cities," in *Art and Life, and the Building and Decoration of Cities* (London, 1897), p. 99. See also Grant Allen, *The British Barbarians: A Hill-Top Novel* (London, 1895), pp. xvii-xviii, and Ernest Dowson, "A Case of Conscience," *Hobby Horse*, No. 21 (January 1891), p. 10.

vegetable matter and unsaleable refuse."[28] Charles Booth's *Life and Labour of the People in London* (13 vols., 1892-1903) dredged forth the mass of unappealing facts; Moore, Crackanthorpe, Hardy, Morrison, Whiteing, and Maugham exploited the vision in fiction. To the creative mind more often than not the brute facts of man's physical nature and oppressive environment connoted "social Darwinism," a world of determined circumstance and no escape.

These are the moods felt and seen in the literature of England from 1880 to 1914. We must keep in mind H. Stuart Hughes' caution against attributing these motifs directly to interinfluence among writers of this time, and against viewing authors of the period as a coherent "school."[29] But the moods are there, visible on the surface; it is my purpose to discover a common cause which may give them coherence and intelligibility. In all their restlessness, vibrancy, excitement, and paradoxical contrariety, these moods bespeak a malaise and loss of hope. The further one reads, the more one suspects that there was some fundamental cause of disillusionment at work, a single challenge to which these varied moods were the response. There are moments of appalled awareness which intrude in this literature, opening a vista of man's ultimate plight in the world he now saw, touched with the note of settled despair. John Eglinton catches that note in his *Two Essays on the Remnant* (1895), where he views civilized man of this time as wrapped in the memories of dreams: "The world is covered with the wrecks of his dream. The

[28] Hardy, *Jude the Obscure* (1895), Pt. III, Chap. 6.
[29] *Consciousness and Society: The Reorientation of European Social Thought,* 1890-1930 (New York: Vintage, 1958), pp. 105-110.

pyramid lies half sunken in the sands; the temple turns yellow on the capes of Greece; the cathedral is a grey presence above the trampling and trundling of the town; within, pictures glow from the roof. Poetry alone, the final art, survives fragmentarily in the slow settling of his mind to contemplation." The contemplation may be wistful, or vacuous, or bitter. For some it brought an impulse to shore, against the ruins of the present, the fragments of a beautiful and believing past—Axel in his castle, Des Esseintes in his house at Fontenay, Oscar Wilde and his blue china.[30] G. K. Chesterton in his *Victorian Age in Literature* (1913), a book of extraordinary staying power for one written so soon after that age had passed, saw the disillusioned years of the *fin de siècle* as "like one long afternoon in a rich house on a rainy day." To another sensibility the sadness is felt as a weariness of the world and of life:

> We have lost
> All hopes we had, all faiths or right or wrong,
> We have been shaken, shattered, tempest-tost,
> And we are weary, and the way is long.[31]

[30] Karl Beckson, in the Introduction to his edition, *Aesthetes and Decadents* (New York: Vintage, 1966), p. xxvii, has an interesting note on the pervasiveness of the image of the hothouse in this period.

[31] Quotations from Chesterton, *The Victorian Age in Literature* (New York: Holt), p. 217; and S. Cornish Watkins, " 'De Profundis,' " *Yellow Book*, III (October 1894), 168; cf. Bernard Capes, "The Accursed Cordonnier," *Dome*, VII (May-July 1900), 101-130; and Oscar Wilde's stanza from "Humanitad":

> Ah! it was easy when the world was young
> To keep one's life free and inviolate,
> From our sad lips another song is rung,
> By our own hands our heads are desecrate.

Through the period, in speculation and in literature, W. H. Mallock's question recurrently arises, "Is life worth living?" In real life, for several poets and artists of the time, the response was "in the negative." The hero of Francis Adams's symptomatic novel, *A Child of the Age*, debates the point: "Was I *never* to have rest, peace, comfort, self-sufficiency, call it what you please,—that spiritual sailing with spread canvas before a full and unvarying wind? *Why* was it, *why?* Was it really because the strange shadow of Purposelessness played the perpetual-rising Banquo at Life's feast for me? Or was it that I was one who could not lack the Personal Deity with impunity? I didn't know, I didn't know! I wished I were dead."[32] *A Child of the Age* first appeared, under a different title, in 1884, nine years before the author's death by suicide.

This was the generation which Yeats (thinking particularly of the 1890s) called back to mind in "The Grey Rock" (1914):

> Poets with whom I learned my trade,
> Companions of the Cheshire Cheese.

He tells them a tale to show that, though man is forever cut off from the gods, to the gods he will still be true: "*I have kept my faith, though faith was tried.*" In 1922 he recalled this generation again and named it tragic, although he was not sure just what had made it so. Was it

---

> Wanderers in drear exile, and dispossessed
> Of what should be our own, we can but feed on
> wild unrest.

[32] (London, 1894), p. 212. Cf. George Egerton, *Discords* (London, 1894), pp. 189-190; M. P. Shiel, *Prince Zaleski* (London, 1895), pp. 143-150; Chesterton, *Autobiography*, p. 337.

that they had lost the "Unity of Being" essential to the artist? Was it the influence of Pater, most of all, who "taught us to walk upon a rope, tightly stretched through serene air," leaving us "to keep our feet upon a swaying rope in a storm"? Or was it "that we lived in what is called 'an age of transition' and so lacked coherence . . . ?"[33]

Beginning? End? Transition? I have already suggested that the British literary culture of the years from 1880 to 1914 was certainly not the end of an epoch, since too many of its moods and doubts are still ours. If it was a transition, the transit is not yet completed. In some larger sense, that age must in fact have been a beginning.

I now turn to the main thesis of this book, that the unity among the myriad moods and motives of the period may best be found by viewing them as varied responses evoked by a single challenge which was posed to man's imaginative life in that time. The following chapter seeks to sketch the nature of that challenge, and the succeeding three chapters suggest the general range of responses made to that challenge. Whether in the result the responses made by these authors were a move forward or a move back is a matter not fully resolved even in our own time. The question of whether beginning, end, or transition becomes one to be asked, not of the period itself, but of the long years since, and of ourselves.

[33] Yeats's general discussion of "The Tragic Generation" appears in *The Trembling of the Veil*, Bk. IV, and these particular quotations in Sects. 3 and 5 of that Book.

CHAPTER 2

The Challenge

Putting the physiological and the barely psychological aspects of the matter aside, what keeps a man alive? What is it that man in his present condition—"too extremely developed," wrote Thomas Hardy in 1889, "for [his] corporeal conditions, the nerves being evolved to an activity abnormal in such an environment"—what is it that man insistently needs to live by?[1] Is it the assurance, which Tennyson and others so often longed for earlier, of something after death? An assurance of some enduring reality "out there" and "not ourselves" to which man can imaginatively or spiritually attach himself? Or is it, more simply, the assurance Jennet Jourdemayne longs for in Christopher Fry's comedy, the

> . . . wish to have some importance
> In the play of time?[2]

Studies of the nineteenth century do not often touch directly on this question, yet the question demands an answer. It must be out of the intellectual and imaginative demands which the Victorians and late-Victorians made on life that many of the moods of the period—skepticism, doubt, anxiety, world-weariness, despair—came into being. Professor Barbara Charlesworth's recent study of the *fin de siècle* suggests that, to stay alive, man's imagination

[1] Florence Emily Hardy, ed., *The Early Life of Thomas Hardy, 1840-91* (New York: Macmillan, 1928), p. 285.
[2] *The Lady's Not for Burning*, Act III.

must have a "belief which will give significance to the moment." Professor Buckley, on the other hand, sees the matter more cheerily, observing that "the late Victorian found that, by a few psychological adjustments, he might continue to live quite comfortably without the support of religion."[3] The late-century crisis was more severe than Professor Buckley's observation suggests. Even in our own time "the problems that the Decadents faced have still no generally accepted solution," and we are still seeking "to discover how literature can become again purposeful and exuberant."[4]

One might argue, along with the behavioral psychologist, that the question is in fact not a matter of intellectual, spiritual, or imaginative needs at all, but simply one of positive reinforcements not given and psychic rewards not received. But the present study takes its evidence from the literature of the time, and the authors of that literature did not feel the crisis in terms of psychological adjustment. It is plain that, in the imaginative life, these decades were felt to be a time of severe deprivation.

The deprivations most keenly felt were two, and they struck at axioms which had long been assumed to be vital

[3] Quotations from Charlesworth, *Dark Passages: The Decadent Consciousness in Victorian Literature* (Madison: University of Wisconsin Press, 1965), p. 122; and Jerome Hamilton Buckley, *William Ernest Henley* (Princeton: Princeton University Press, 1945), p. 25. Professor Buckley has perhaps modified his view when he speaks of "the intensity, the self-effacement, the high seriousness," required to produce great art. (*The Victorian Temper: A Study in Literary Culture*, 1st edn. 1951 [New York: Random House, 1964], p. 234.)

[4] Quotations from Charlesworth, *Dark Passages*, p. 123; and Colin Wilson, *The Strength to Dream* (Boston: Houghton Mifflin, 1962), p. xx.

if existence was to have significance. The first axiom held that somewhere within or behind or beyond the world of observable experience there was an eternal and credible truth, a truth accordant to, at least consistent with, the human spirit and its aspirations. The second axiom held that man possessed a faculty capable of at least dimly perceiving that truth. If the predicament which faced the new age can be stated in its simplest terms at the outset, it can be said in the words of E. M. Forster: "Both assumptions are false: both of them must be accepted as true if we are to go on eating and working and loving, and are to keep open a few breathing holes for the human spirit." Man's environment seemed less and less to reflect man's humanity and to grow more and more hostile to it, while at the same time man's ability to comprehend his environment seemed to decrease. And "unless man have a natural bent in accordance with nature's," wrote Charles S. Pierce, "he has no chance of understanding nature at all."[5]

To know that there is an eternal truth consonant to man's being, and to know that man is gifted with a faculty capable of perceiving at least a glimmer of that truth —these were the necessary axioms, and both were, or appeared to be, substantially demolished in the years between 1880 and 1914.

To the first axiom the challenge came primarily from the advance of science and its implied cosmology. The

[5] Quotations from Forster, "What I Believe," in *Two Cheers for Democracy*, p. 71; the consistency of Forster's world-view from first to last justifies this excerpt from an essay of 1939; and Pierce, "A Neglected Argument for the Reality of God," *Hibbert Journal*, VII (1908-1909), p. 106.

story has been often told, of the work of Lyell in geology, Strauss and Renan in the higher criticism of the Bible, Wallace and Darwin in biology, and the rest. By the end of the century the main features of the challenge were manifest to every observant mind. There had been a crescendo of scientific observations and theories which seemed to prove finally that man was not a special creation, that he was rather a product of external and predetermined terrestrial forces, and forever cut off from a heaven or a haven of absolutes corresponding to human aspirations. Doubt and ambiguity as to man's position in the scheme of things had been felt keenly enough in the earlier decades.[6] In the late century the assaults of scientific theory on human dignity and spiritual aspiration had become more closely coordinated and more devastating, seemingly linked into a single refutation of all which man's imagination had lived by:

> Which was it of the links
> Snapt first, from out the chain which used to bind
> Our earth to heaven . . . ?[7]

—so Browning could ask in 1887. But well before this time the scientists had gathered confidence that with them lay the answer; their voices became more strident and dogmatic, as did John Tyndall's toward the close of his famous

[6] Good accounts are given in Walter E. Houghton, *The Victorian Frame of Mind: 1830-1870* (New Haven: Yale University Press, 1957), pp. 9-23, 261-262, and J. Hillis Miller, *The Disappearance of God: Five Nineteenth-Century Writers* (Cambridge: Harvard University Press, 1963), p. 13.

[7] "Parleyings with Gerard de Lairesse" (1887), quoted in Miller, *Disappearance of God*, p. 99.

Belfast Address (1874): "The impregnable position of science may be described in a few words. We claim, and we shall wrest from theology, the entire domain of cosmological theory. All schemes and systems which thus infringe upon the domain of science must, in so far as they do this, submit to its control, and relinquish all thought of controlling it." By the 1880s the theologian himself might well be driven to capitulate: "There is a sense of solidity about a Law of Nature which belongs to nothing else in the world."[8] A net of fixed laws and consequences already seemed to be closing around man's existence, moving in from the Newtonian universe to inanimate nature on earth, and now, through the laws of political economy and biology, to the life of man himself.[9] Earlier phases of Victorian doubt had been read as transitional, the darkness before a dawn which was certain to break.[10] Carlyle's "universe . . . all void of Life, of Purpose, of Volition, even of Hostility" was torment

[8] Henry Drummond, *Natural Law in the Spiritual World*, 1st edn. 1883 (London, 1889), p. xxiii.

[9] In the years since, the trajectory of scientific advance (giving perhaps too little credit to the influence of eighteenth-century rationalism and early nineteenth-century positivism) has been often described: "Newton banished God from nature, Darwin banished him from life, Freud drove him from the last fastness, the Soul" (Gerald Heard, quoted in Jacques Barzun, *Darwin, Marx, Wagner* [2nd edn., New York: Doubleday, 1958], p. 87). Cf. Llewellyn Powys, quoted in H. G. Wood, *Belief and Unbelief Since 1850* (Cambridge, Eng.: Cambridge University Press, 1955), pp. 58-59; Floyd Dell, quoted in Frederick J. Hoffman, *Freudianism and the Literary Mind* (New York: Grove, 1959), p. 72.

[10] The early Victorian's view of his time as "an age of transition" is well documented in Houghton, *Victorian Frame of Mind*, Chap. 1.

enough—but a firm *Apage Satana*! could at last dispel the demon.[11] By the late century the web of circumstance had drawn in with finality. Man had been asked to sit down before the fact like a little child; he had for decades viewed with acquiescence and respect, and at times with exhilaration, the triumphs of science in the industrial age. Now the cosmology implicit in the new science began to assume coherence and came starkly into view. It revealed man helplessly enmeshed by inhuman and impersonal forces in a world he never made and could not control, caught up in a life of no purpose, neither human nor ethical nor divine—

> While the sad waters of separation
> Bear us on to the ultimate night.

The scientist's description of the newfound reality becomes explicit and exclusive: "[We are] convinced . . . that truth unadulterated is only to be found in the temple of the study of nature . . ."; ". . . It ought to be known and avowed that the physical philosopher, as such, must be a pure materialist"; and ". . . Science . . . as habitually taken . . . is identified with . . . the belief that the hidden order of nature is mechanical exclusively."[12] The truth had proved to be radically inhuman. Man's existence had

[11] Carlyle, *Sartor Resartus*, Bk. II, Chap. 7.

[12] The lines of poetry and the three subsequent quotations are from Ernest Dowson, "Exile" (1896); Ernst Haeckel, *The Riddle of the Universe* (English trans., 1901), Chap. 18; John Tyndall, "Matter and Force," in *Fragments of Science* (2 vols., London, 1879), II, 72; and William James, *The Will to Believe and Other Essays in Popular Philosophy* (New York, 1903), pp. 323-324. Cf. H. Stuart Hughes (*Consciousness and Society* [New York: Random House, 1958], p. 31), quotations from Roger Martin du Gard.

become "an accident, his story a brief and transitory episode in the life of one of the meanest of the planets."[13]

More than this, the new view of man's cosmos struck just as directly at the second axiom of man's imaginative life. It proposed that empirical observation and inductive logic were man's only sure routes toward this ultimate, inhuman truth, and it would admit no other cognitive faculties than these. Again let the voices of the new science speak: ". . . Physical theories which lie beyond experience are derived by a process of abstraction from experience"; ". . . That dry light of reason . . . is the sole human test of truth"; ". . . Logic, after all, has always the last word here below"; and "Emotion has nothing whatever to do with the attainment of truth."[14]

Statements like these may seem relatively innocuous, but I believe they point to a sharp constriction of the faculty of reason in this generation from that conceived in earlier years of the nineteenth century. When Matthew Arnold speaks of reason, he is thinking of the reason of the great humanistic tradition; he indicates as much explicitly in his occasional phrase, "right reason." When John Morley argues for "mental detachment," he acknowledges simultaneously "the supreme claim of the individual conscience," again implying a necessary alliance of intellect

[13] Arthur James Balfour, *The Foundations of Belief* (London, 1895), p. 30.

[14] The four quotations are from Tyndall, "Belfast Address," Sect. 8 in *Fragments of Science*, II, 190; "Dr. Temple on Religion and Science," anonymous article in *Westminster Review*, LXVII (April 1885), 366; Marie Jean Guyau, *The Non-Religion of the Future* (London, 1897), p. 20; and Haeckel, *Riddle of the Universe*, p. 17. The growing assumption that man has but one faculty for knowing truth probably encouraged the inclination toward monism at the end of the century.

with other modes of cognition.[15] Even with Mill the reason bears the dignity of a faculty which can enlighten morals and conduct as well as physical phenomena and laws. Professor Houghton wisely engages extensively, in his *Victorian Frame of Mind*, with the Victorian reliance upon reason, for the early and mid-Victorian shapers of culture had a high confidence in that faculty—hedged around as it was with appeals to the intuition, the "illative sense," the *Aberglaube*.

What happened in the late century was that reason became narrowed, hardened, crystallized out into a single, rigorously disciplined faculty—crystallized out, in short, into the scientific method as the sole source of "a sound view of the world." Little wonder then that as human reason was thus trimmed down to such a constricted and efficient method, it should have been felt more and more that spiritual aspirations fell "quite outside the province of rational belief." Worse than this, and completely unperceived by most minds of the time, the faculty of reason, thus limited, stepped into a trap and was hoist with its own petard. "Reason is naturally monist," as Unamuno was to say. As the reason was reduced to a method which could deal only with sensible, quantifiable experience within a single system of laws that were assumed to be entirely predictable, the reality behind phenomena to which it could attain was simultaneously confined to a reality inducible from material sensations and operating within a closed field of causes and predictable effects. "The Eye altering alters all," perversely to quote William Blake.[16]

[15] *Recollections* (2 vols., New York: Macmillan, 1917), I, 21-22.
[16] The quotations in the paragraph derive, respectively, from

In its capitulation to "that dry light" of scientific inquiry, the human mind haplessly abandoned both axioms at once; by placing all faith in such a narrow faculty of cognition, it accepted in advance an inhospitable and deterministic view of the ultimate truth, the only view, by definition, to which such a method could lead. The shades of monism drew in. With remarkable prescience, Dostoevsky's man underground foresaw this result in 1864: "After all, if desire should at any time come to terms completely with reason, we shall then, of course, reason and not desire...."[17] With the mechanical monism of Ernst Haeckel and his allies, Dostoevsky's fears would appear to have come true.

In such a line of reasoning, the needs of the aspiring imagination were frontally thwarted by a triumphant scientific method and a bleak ultimate reality—a conflict rendered none the more pleasant by its being a war not between good and evil, but between two goods, man's spiritual and imaginative life and "the truth." As Haeckel saw it—speaking here of the Catholic faith in particular—it was a war to the death: "The modern papacy, true to the despotic principles it has followed for the last sixteen

---

Havelock Ellis, *The Dance of Life* (London: Constable, 1923), p. 199; Henry C. Sheldon, *Unbelief in the Nineteenth Century* (London: Charles Kelly, n.d.), p. 42; Miguel de Unamuno, *Tragic Sense of Life,* trans. J. E. Crawford Flitch (New York: Dover, 1954), p. 80; and William Blake, "The Mental Traveller" (circ. 1803).

[17] Fyodor Dostoevsky, *Notes from Underground and The Grand Inquisitor*, trans. Ralph E. Matlaw (New York: Dutton, 1960), p. 24. *The Monist* journal began publication in Chicago in 1890; see especially the article "Our Monism," II (July 1892), 481-486. See also A. Worsley, *Concepts of Monism* (London, 1907).

hundred years, is determined to wield sole dominion over the credulous souls of men; it must demand the absolute submission of the cultured State, which, as such, defends the rights of reason and science. True and enduring peace there cannot be until one of the combatants lies powerless on the ground." Havelock Ellis provides a characteristic record of the impact of the conflict on a sensitive mind in the 1870s and '8os: ". . . I had the feeling that the universe was represented as a sort of factory filled by an inextricable web of wheels and looms and flying shuttles, in a deafening din. That, it seemed, was the world as the most competent scientific authorities declared it to be made. It was a world I was prepared to accept and yet a world in which, I felt, I could only wander restlessly, an ignorant and homeless child."[18] One might well cry out with Kent in *King Lear*, "Is this the promised end?" One can find empathy at least for the diagnosis offered by Thomas Hardy's doctor on the murders and the suicide committed by the young Jude Fawley: ". . . It is the beginning of the coming universal wish not to live."[19]

Now Ernst Haeckel's was a clear mind, a confident and a consistent mind; yet to our twentieth-century view, as we look back on this forthright solution to the riddle of the universe, it seems most surely to have been a superficial mind. Its bleak conclusions could hardly seem more dated than they seem now. And it is when we ask *why* they seem so dated that we come to the second major

[18] Haeckel, *Riddle of the Universe*, p. 335; and Ellis, *Dance of Life*, p. 199. It is not surprising that literature in this period often speaks in cosmic terms, of dynasts and the Will, the eternity of earth, and the Life Force; the challenge of scientific determinism had cosmic implications.

[19] Hardy, *Jude the Obscure* (1895), Pt. VI, Chap. 2.

phase of the challenge posed to the culture of the years between 1880 and 1914. One reason for the antique air of Haeckel's thought is that such arrant determinism simply contradicts our daily experience of purposive action. Haeckel fits perfectly Whitehead's caricature of the scientist who "has patiently designed experiments for the *purpose* of substantiating his belief that animal operations are motivated by no purposes."[20] But much more than this, Haeckel's datedness stems from the fact that, even as he wrote, the nature of science and the world it revealed were radically changing. The Roentgen ray, natural radioactivity, the Fitz-Gerald contraction, the special theory of relativity, and the quantum theory were all discoveries and hypotheses of the 1890s and early 1900s.

Each in its own way called into question the fixed certainties of Haeckelian science; with the full authority of the scientific method, each found flexibility and uncertainty lurking in the Victorian's concepts of time and space, motion and matter, and the predictability of scientific laws. In retrospect we can see that the age of relativity, of statistics and probabilities, of symbols and uncertainty principles was beginning to set in. A strikingly clear and early voice to express the new direction in science is found in Karl Pearson, whose *Grammar of Science* appeared in 1892. We can catch the accent of the work most succinctly in the response of Henry Adams, on whom it had strong influence: "Pearson shut out of science everything which the nineteenth century had brought into it. He told his scholars that they must put up with a fraction of the universe, and a very small frac-

[20] Alfred North Whitehead, *The Function of Reason* (Princeton: Princeton University Press, 1929), Chap. 1.

tion at that—the circle reached by the senses, where sequence could be taken for granted—much as the deep-sea fish takes for granted the circle of light which he generates." Provided with such a striking clue from the theorist of science, we become aware that the same notion was entering the literary consciousness as well. George Gissing had concluded seven years before that "it is ill to have been born in these times, but one can make a world within a world." Conrad was later to announce that "in truth every novelist must begin by creating for himself a world, great or little, in which he can honestly believe."[21]

To measure the distance we have traveled from earlier views of "the truth," consider this from one born about two decades before Gissing and Conrad: "They who tamper with veracity, from whatever motive, are tampering with the vital force of human progress.... Anything that turns the edge of reason fatally blunts the surest and most potent of our weapons."[22] More and more toward the close of the 1880-1914 period, literary minds sensed that science had moved into a new phase. The certainties had become uncertain; man was called on to live not so much with a world of materialistic determinism, as with a

[21] Quotations from *The Education of Henry Adams* (1907), Chap. 31; Jacob Korg, *George Gissing: A Critical Biography* (Seattle: University of Washington Press, 1963), p. 92; and Conrad, "Books" (1905), in Walter F. Wright, ed., *Joseph Conrad on Fiction* (Lincoln: University of Nebraska Press, 1964), p. 79. See also H. V. Routh, *Towards the Twentieth Century* (New York: Methuen, 1937), p. 361.

[22] John Morley, *On Compromise* (1886), concluding paragraph of Chap. 3, quoted in Buckley, *The Victorian Temper*, headnote to Chap. 10.

world of chance and change within which man had now to grope his way in uncertainty. Edward Carpenter could ask in 1916, "Where *are* the airy fairy laws and theories of the Science of the last century? . . . All gone into the melting-pot—and quickly losing their outlines." The *real* world in which man lived became more remote and difficult—perhaps impossible—to *know*. "Chance now became the basis of a new scientific logic," wrote Stow Persons. "The individual particle or person was thus left partially undetermined as to the laws of its behavior." We have moved to the world of which Max Planck could say, "As the view of the physical world is perfected, it simultaneously recedes from the world of sense."[23]

One thought that appalled the imagination of this time was that behind all the phenomena perceptible to human senses there might lie—NOTHING. Perhaps all the world man knew was blank and void at the heart. James (B.V.) Thomson had had his own inferno to endure and had faced the specter of nothingness:

[23] The quotations are from Carpenter, *My Days and Dreams* (London: Allen and Unwin, 1916), Chap. 11; Persons, "Darwinism and American Culture," in *The Impact of Darwinian Thought on American Life and Culture* (Austin: University of Texas, 1959), p. 7; and Planck, *The Universe in the Light of Modern Physics* (London: Allen and Unwin, 1931), p. 14. To a later and better-informed synthesizer of literary culture, Planck's statement may suggest a distinct new trend in the literary imagination of the twentieth century; the scientist's cosmology may have receded so far from the layman's comprehension that *l'homme moyen littéraire* is left with no "real" cosmology at all on which to draw or rely. Perhaps Professor J. Hillis Miller's excellent study of "the disappearance of God" in the nineteenth century may be matched, one day in the future, by a study of "the disappearance of the universe" in the twentieth.

The sense that every struggle brings defeat
　Because Fate holds no prize to crown success;
That all the oracles are dumb and cheat
　Because they have no secret to express.

The Cyrenaicism of Pater's Marius also "had left off in
suspense of judgment as to what might really lie behind
. . . the flaming ramparts of the world." Oscar Wilde
wrote of the timelessly wise sphinx—without a secret.
Baudelaire and Dowson sensed a nothingness at the heart
of things; Conrad's Kurtz was revealed horribly to be
"hollow at the core"; and John Davidson found nothing
at the root of life, which made it "an inexorable irony."[24]
One might pursue the theme closer to our time when
the hero of Zamiatin's *We* looks up to the heavens: "The
ancients 'knew' that the greatest, bored skeptic—their
god—lived there. We know that crystalline, blue, naked,
indecent Nothing is there." Hemingway encountered his
nada, George Orwell his "deadly emptiness . . . at the
heart of things," and Jean-Paul Sartre his awareness that
behind all appearance "there is nothing."[25] The percep-

[24] Quotations from Thomson, "The City of Dreadful Night"
(1874), Sect. 21; Pater, *Marius*, Chap. 8; Conrad, *Heart of Darkness* (1898), Pt. III; and Davidson, "Recent Views of Poetry,"
Speaker (March 4, 1899), p. 260. See also Davidson's *The Theatrocrat* (1905), p. 27; Nietzsche: "There is no 'being' behind
doing, acting, becoming" (*Genealogy of Morals* [English trans.,
1899], First Essay, Sect. 13); and Archibald MacLeish, "The
End of the World" (1926):
　　　"There in the sudden blackness the black pall
　　　Of nothing, nothing, nothing—nothing at all."
[25] Eugene Zamiatin, *We*, (1924) trans. Gregory Zilboorg (New
York: Dutton, 1959), "Record Eleven," second paragraph; George
Orwell, *A Clergyman's Daughter* (London: Secker and Warburg,
1960), p. 315; and Sartre, *Nausea* (1938), trans. Lloyd Alexander
(New York: New Directions, 1959), p. 131.

tions prompted by the stress of these years at the turn of the century are prophetic of moods familiar to us today.

Such changes in the nature of the physical world also meant the revision of man's view of his faculties of cognition. Karl Pearson and Arthur Balfour foresaw the needed revision early in the 1890s; Balfour himself suggested that the mind, on naturalistic terms, be regarded "as an instrument for securing a flexibility of adaptation which instinct alone is not able to attain." But the best description of the role of the mind in the new world of science is that given by Hans Vaihinger: "It must be remembered that the object of the world of ideas as a whole is not the portrayal of reality—this would be an utterly impossible task—but rather to provide us with an *instrument for finding our way about more easily in this world. . . .* [The logical function] *. . . provisionally substitutes for the correct constructs others which do not directly correspond to reality. . . .* [Thus these constructs] *. . . deliberately substitute a fraction of reality for the complete range of causes and facts.*"[26]

The human mind on these terms moves like the groping tentacle of the snail probing into the darkness, coming somehow to terms with the task of survival in its environment. It moves not by the light of knowing the nature of a cause-and-effect universe in which it lives, but experimentally, pragmatically, and by chance. Once this

[26] Quotations from Balfour, *Foundations of Belief*, Chap. 3 (see also Pearson, *Grammar of Science* [1892], Chap. 2); and Vaihinger, *The Philosophy of 'As If,'* trans. C. K. Ogden (London: Routledge and Kegan Paul, 1924), pp. 15, 17, 20. Vaihinger's views took shape in 1874-1876, his book was published in German in 1911 and in English in 1924. William Barrett, *Irrational Man* (New York: Doubleday, 1958), Chap. 1, touches on the influence of this view of the mind's limitations on existentialist thought.

new conception of the human mind has been detected, one can see that it was indeed weaving its way into the thought and culture of this period and of the decades that followed. As early as 1893 F. H. Bradley concluded that "my external sensations are no less private to myself than are my thoughts or my feelings. In either case my experience falls within my own circle, a circle closed on the outside. . . . In brief . . . the whole world for each is peculiar and private to that soul." Santayana picks up the motif in his early poetry—"Truth is a dream, unless my dream is true"—and in his later speculations in *Scepticism and Animal Faith* of man "blindly labouring in a blind world." The way has been paved for Mrs. Ramsay's question in *To the Lighthouse*: "How then," she had asked herself, "did one know one thing or another thing about people, sealed as they were? Only like a bee. . . ." And, still closer to our time, the motif leads to the closed field of Samuel Beckett's world: "Murphy's mind pictured itself as a large hollow sphere, hermetically closed to the universe without. . . . Nothing had ever been, was or would be in the universe outside it but was already present as virtual, or actual, or virtual rising into actual, or actual falling into virtual, in the universe inside it."[27]

So it is manifest, turning back to our 1880-1914 period, that Darwinian evolution, which had seemed so deterministic, contained after all "suggestions of a way of

[27] The quotations are from Bradley, *Appearance and Reality: A Metaphysical Essay* (2nd edn., London, 1908), p. 346; George Santayana, Sonnet V from the sequence of 1883-1893, in *Poems* (New York: Scribner's, 1923), p. 7, and his *Scepticism and Animal Faith* (1923) (New York: Dover, 1955), p. 52; Virginia Woolf, *To the Lighthouse* (1927) (New York: Harcourt, Brace and World, n.d.), p. 79; and Beckett, *Murphy* (New York: Grove, 1957), p. 107.

viewing events quite at variance with the mechanistic root-metaphor of the scientific revolution." And the most that our noblest spokesman for human reason in recent years will grant to that faculty is "an asymptotic approach to the truth."[28]

But the point needs now to be made that these new views of the cosmos and of man's faculty of cognition posed a challenge to his spiritual and imaginative life which was scarcely less severe than that posed by the earlier materialism. This new view of a world of flux locked man within his own world of sense impressions, with no hope at all of a real or credible world behind sensed phenomena and, even if there were such a world, no means—not even the scientist's logic—which could perceive or envision it. The two basic axioms were denied again. Life came to be like that described with extraordinary prescience and influence by Walter Pater in 1868: "Experience, already reduced to a group of impressions, is ringed round for each one of us by that thick wall of personality through which no real voice has ever pierced on its way to us, or from us to that which we can only conjecture to be without. Every one of those impressions is the impression of the individual in his isolation, each mind keeping as a solitary prisoner its own dream of a world."[29]

Having glanced ahead to the later consequences of this estimate of human consciousness, we must recognize that

[28] The two quotations are from James Street Fulton, "Philosophical Adventures of the Idea of Evolution: 1859-1959," *Rice Institute Pamphlet*, XLVI (April 1959), 4; and Whitehead, *Function of Reason*, p. 53. Cf. Ellis, *Dance of Life*, p. 94.

[29] "Conclusion," *Renaissance*; see also Milton Millhauser, "Walter Pater and the Flux," *JAAC*, XI (March 1953), 214-223.

there had been premonitions of it before in Victorian literature—in Tennyson's "Palace of Art," in William Morris, and notably in D. G. Rossetti: "All my life I have dreamt one dream alone."[30] But the characteristic earlier response to this view was to subdue the artist's dream and to return to the realm of duty, work, and action. Pater himself, by withdrawing his "Conclusion" from the second edition (1877) of *The Renaissance*, demonstrated his own uncertainty as to whether his concept of human consciousness was the true one or the right one for his age. But Pater's disciples and successors accepted it with confidence and as a shaping force in the aestheticism of this period. Pater's judgment had its value and sustenance, and its dangers. Professor Charlesworth's perceptive study of the period sees the view as becoming solipsistic and imprisoning to the creative artist, an invitation to decadence: ". . . The poets of the nineties perished there, not because they 'found a haven in the world' but because in the specious haven of their own imaginations they slept away their days. They desired moments of heightened consciousness, of imaginative insight, 'simply,' as Pater advised in the 'Conclusion,' 'for those moments' sake.' By doing so, they robbed such moments of all significance, narrowed them into the circle of the individual consciousness, and, destroying the possibility of vision, brought them wholly into the realm of dream."[31]

In later literary culture it might be argued that this second phase of the challenge, premised on flux rather than on fixity, on probing in the darkness rather than on the

[30] Oswald Doughty, *A Victorian Romantic: Dante Gabriel Rossetti* (London: Frederick Muller, 1949), p. 347.

[31] *Dark Passages*, p. 122.

36

cold logic of the empirical-inductive method, was less devastating. The writings of William Butler Yeats and James Joyce show what heights literature could achieve on the new terms. Yet the dubious battle still continues. Perhaps, as there has always been Platonist versus Aristotelian, there will always be those who seize avidly on the loopholes in a materialistic system and regard each loophole found as an affirmation of man's spiritual life. What emerges clearly in the culture of this period is the conclusion that if deterministic materialism left no room for the human imagination and spirit, the new vistas of relativity offered little better. Walter Houghton observes of the earlier Victorians that they "might be, and often were, uncertain about what theory to accept or what faculty to rely on; but it never occurred to them to doubt their capacity to arrive at truth."[32] By the close of the period we are considering, the moment of ultimate doubt *had* arrived. The world of "truth" had become shadowy and fluctuating at best; man's ability to perceive it had diminished toward the vanishing point.

It will help to clarify and extend our picture of this complex two-part, two-phase challenge of the years at the turn of the century if we consider one major example of that challenge at work—the Darwinian theory of evolution by means of natural selection. Few people now, it may be hoped, think of Charles Darwin as the discoverer and "onlie begetter" of the theory of evolution. What he did was to gather into focus much existent speculation on the subject, theories that seemed to "float like rumours" in the air at mid-century. With meticulous care and method, and marshaling vast amounts of data, he moved "over

[32] *Victorian Frame of Mind*, p. 14.

the subject with the passionless strength of a glacier."[33]
In the result he convinced the world less of the validity
of his main point—mutational development of species by
natural selection—than of the whole concept of evolution
upon which that thesis was based. That concept, in its
large outlines, has not been widely or seriously questioned
since Darwin's time.

It is hard for us to recapture now the devastating impact of *The Origin of Species* in 1859 and the years just
after. To the speculative mind it seemed the final intrusion of mechanistic science into the *sanctum sanctorum*
of man's inner being. It caught up living man in the
meshes of the cause and effect of the physical world. To
the literary imagination the concept of evolution clung
with the additional tenacity of a central metaphor, something like that of the great chain of being in the neoclas-
sical tradition or the concept of organism with the Romantics. There was scarcely any mode of thinking, ethical,
spiritual, or aesthetic, which did not have to reckon now
with the fact and the metaphor of evolution. Evolution
was one of several theories which drew the literary mind
of this period to dwell recurrently on the ultimate nature
of human life, to brood upon the cosmos, and to view
man's condition *sub specie aeternitatis*.

The first effect of *The Origin of Species* was to precipitate and dramatize the clash between science and religion. This is the impact most often recorded in social
and intellectual histories dealing with this time—Huxley's
masterly retort to Bishop Wilberforce in the Oxford de-

[33] Quotations from John Tyndall, "Science and Man," in *Fragments*, II, 340; and Tyndall, "Belfast Address," in *ibid.*, II, 181.
See also David G. Ritchie, *Darwin and Hegel* (London, 1893),
pp. 41ff.

bate of June 1860, or Disraeli in the *Punch* cartoon, be-
winged and self-admiring, repeating his Oxford contention, ". . . I am on the side of the angels."[34]

As early as 1853 the Goncourts had written in their *Journal, "Chaque jour, la science mange du Dieu."* The scientists themselves often longed wistfully for the higher faith
and for the ethical process which had been exiled from
their materialistic cosmos, but which Darwinism seemed
finally to have cast out. Darwin's consolation in the *The
Origin of Species*—"I see no good reason why the views
given in this volume should shock the religious feelings
of any one"—must itself be taken in conjunction with his
later view: "The mystery of the beginning of all things
is insoluble by us; and I for one must be content to remain
an Agnostic."[35] The scientific work of Tyndall and Huxley was marked also by a longing for a higher truth and
a basis for ethics, and deep qualms of conscience lest the
new science may have eroded such ground away.[36] As evidence that the fear of science's assault on religion was
widespread and deep in the popular conscience toward the
close of the century, witness the nearly 2,000 correspond-

[34] Leonard Huxley, ed., *Life and Letters of Thomas Henry Huxley* (2 vols., New York, 1900), I, 192-204, gives a full account of
the Oxford debate; and *Punch*, XLVI (December 10, 1864), 239.

[35] Quotations from Edmond and Jules de Goncourt, *Journal:
Memoires de la vie littéraire* (22 vols., Monaco: Imprimerie Na-
tionale, 1956), I, 110; Charles Darwin, "Conclusion," *Origin of
Species*; and Darwin's letter to a German student, 1879, in Francis
Darwin, ed., *The Life and Letters of Charles Darwin* (2 vols.,
New York, 1888), I, 282. Regarding the corrosive effect of scien-
tific labor on Darwin's aesthetic sense, see *ibid.*, I, 81.

[36] John Tyndall, "The Rev. James Martineau and the Belfast
Address," *Fragments*, II, 232, and Thomas Henry Huxley's essay,
"Evolution and Ethics" (1892).

ents who engaged in the controversy, "Is Christianity Played out?" which ran in the columns of the London *Daily Chronicle* from January 14 to January 31, 1893, at which date it had to be terminated by editorial command. The agnosticism to which Darwin resorted—and Huxley, and Leslie Stephen, and others—brought little real spiritual consolation; it is difficult to muster fervency in the worship of the Unknowable. Beatrice Webb quickly sensed that agnostic philosophy "destroys all our present grounds for believing in immortality, in any being higher than humanity. . . . There is little doubt that at present this philosophy darkens the life of man."[37] And lest we regard this whole "Darwin *vs.* religion" controversy as so hackneyed now that it must have been the result of a misconceived metaphysic or an antiquated terminology, it is well to recall Julian Huxley's words, spoken on the eve of the Darwinian centenary: ". . . If evolution is accepted as a fact, much of the *theological* framework of the world's major religions is destroyed. . . ."[38]

The dark response to Darwinism ran quickly beyond theological bounds to cosmic pessimism and "through Science to despair" in the later century.[39] It appears even in such passing comments as a reviewer's judgment of

[37] MS diary, September 22, 1881, in *My Apprenticeship* (London: Longmans, Green, 1926), p. 88. Cf. William James, "The Sentiment of Rationality" (1880), in *The Will to Believe*: "There can be no greater incongruity than for a disciple of Spencer to proclaim with one breath that the substance of things is unknowable, and with the next that the thought of it should inspire us with awe, reverence. . . ."

[38] "Darwin and the Idea of Evolution" (1958), in *Darwin and His Critics*, ed. Bernard R. Kogan (San Francisco: Wadsworth, 1960), p. 137.

[39] George Meredith, "Foresight and Patience" (1894).

Jude the Obscure: "If these men and women and their companions are to be taken as true to modern life, we may as well accept a cage full of monkeys as a microcosm of humanity."[40] Man was now thought of as the helpless pawn of the Malthusian biological drives of sex and hunger and caught up, in defiance of the first axiom, in a "reality" utterly inhuman and wholly unresponsive to his spiritual or imaginative aspirations. Hardy describes in this fashion the attraction which Arabella holds for Jude Fawley: "In short, as if materially, a compelling arm of extraordinary muscular power seized hold of him—something which had nothing in common with the spirits and influences that had moved him hitherto. This seemed to care little for his reason and his will, nothing for his so-called elevated intentions. . . ."[41]

Darwin left no room whatever for purpose in the world, human or divine, or for any free will to pursue such a purpose if there was one. He posited only, in the infinitely remote past, an initiating First Cause. Thereafter, the impersonal, predetermined, external forces of the material world shaped all that man has become and can be. There was no room for humanity, only brute struggle for survival, and survival only of the fittest. "From such beginnings," wrote Balfour, "famine, disease, and mutual slaughter, fit nurses of the future lords of creation, have gradually evolved, after infinite travail, a race with conscience enough to feel that it is vile, and intelligence enough to know that it is insignificant." Since the im-

---

[40] Quoted in Carl J. Weber, *Hardy of Wessex: His Life and Literary Career* (New York: Columbia University Press, 1940), p. 149.

[41] *Jude the Obscure*, Pt. I, Chap. 7.

plications of Darwinism invaded all regions of human thought, the "gladiatorial theory of existence" invaded man's social thinking as well and, in the form of social Darwinism, gave Karl Marx "a basis in natural science for the class struggle in history," and gave Herbert Spencer grounds for seeing "a large, far-seeing benevolence" in the "poverty of the incapable, . . . the starvation of the idle."[42]

There were attempts to counter and reverse the pressure of Darwinism toward a pessimistic view of man's condition. Darwin himself, with characteristic utter caution, proposed that "man may be excused for feeling some pride at having risen, though not through his own exertions, to the very summit of the organic scale; and the fact of his having thus risen, instead of having been aboriginally placed there, may give him hope for a still higher destiny in the distant future."[43] Optimism of this sort had been associated with evolution in earlier decades, viewing "the history of animal life as a great progressive development from the amoeba up through fishes to reptiles, to birds, to mammals, culminating . . . in man. But need it stop there?"[44] But such optimism lost much of its force in the later century. Of Darwin's own statement, one might well ask how man is to take pride in advances

[42] Quotations from Balfour, *Foundations of Belief*, p. 30; Huxley, "Evolution and Ethics"; Marx's letter to Friedrich Engels, as quoted in Kogan, ed., *Darwin and His Critics*, p. 166; and Spencer, *Social Statics* (1850), cited in Houghton, *Victorian Frame of Mind*, p. 209.

[43] *The Descent of Man and Selection in Relation to Sex* (1871), concluding paragraph; see also "Recapitulation and Conclusion" in his *Origin of Species*.

[44] Houghton, *Victorian Frame of Mind*, p. 36; see also *ibid.*, pp. 37, 250. See also Buckley, *Victorian Temper*, p. 174.

achieved "not through his own exertions"? If it is spiritual exaltation Darwin means to offer us, we are once again confronted with the difficulty of worshipping a First Cause present 500,000,000 years ago and absent ever since.

A more fully articulated case for optimism in evolution was advanced by the neo-Lamarckians, best expressed in literature in the works of Samuel Butler and George Bernard Shaw. This line of reasoning and the course it followed at the turn of the century will be discussed in more detail later (pp. 81 ff.) when I consider the responses of the mind to the challenge of this time. At present, only two things need be said. Neo-Lamarckianism based its argument on the inheritance of acquired characteristics; if new and higher characteristics could be acquired by one generation and then transmitted to the next, then man could once again seize some control of his own destiny and assist the Life Force on its upward course. But it became clear, even during the 1880-1914 period, that the findings of science were moving steadily against the neo-Lamarckians and demonstrating that acquired characteristics *cannot* be inherited, and that any notion of an *élan vital* as a separate force ran counter to science's commitment to mechanistic monism. As Thomas Huxley wryly observed, those who ascribe evolution to an *élan vital* might as well speak of an *élan locomotif* to explain the workings of a steam engine.[45] By 1914, Darwinian evolution had clearly won the day and had retained its force as prime mover in science's shaping of a materialistic, deterministic, blindly purposeless world.

But here, just as with the challenge of science as a

[45] George Gaylord Simpson, *The Meaning of Evolution* (New Haven: Yale University Press, 1952), p. 273.

whole, there is a change in the direction of Darwinian controversy in the later years of the 1880-1914 period. Exactitude in chronology does not apply here; the responses to Darwinism vary in date and intensity largely in accordance with the cast and perceptivity of the individual imagination. Yet even in the 1890s there are signs of a perplexing pause and a waning of intensity in the science-religion conflict itself. Was it simply what Esmé Wingfield-Stratford calls "the influence of boredom on the course of history"—had man simply talked himself out on the subject of Darwinism?[46] Or must we settle for H. G. Wells's cryptic acceptance of the time as "full of the ironical silences that follow great controversies"? Whatever brought it about, there was an impression abroad that "the long-standing feud between theology and science was at last practically ended."[47]

[46] Wingfield-Stratford, *The Victorian Sunset* (New York: William Morrow, 1932), p. 144. The suggestion is an affront to human reason. Suzanne K. Langer's view (*Philosophy in a New Key* [Cambridge, Mass.: Harvard University Press, 1942], p. 23) is somewhat kinder: "The sudden vogue of . . . a key-idea is due to the fact that all sensitive and active minds turn at once to exploiting it; we try it in every connection, for every purpose, experiment with possible stretches of its strict meaning, with generalizations and derivatives. When we become familiar with the new idea our expectations do not outrun its actual uses quite so far, and then its unbalanced popularity is over."

[47] Quotations from Wells, in G. K. Chesterton, *Autobiography* (London: Hutchinson, 1937), p. 144, and from W. Sanday, "Professor Huxley as a Theologian," *Contemporary Review*, LXII (September 1892), 337. Cf. Alfred North Whitehead, *Science and the Modern World* (New York: Macmillan, 1931), p. 96: "Suddenly, a pause occurred; and in its last twenty years the century closed with one of the dullest stages of thought since the time of the First Crusade."

Just as the larger challenge in this culture shifted its direction in the later years of the period between 1880 and 1914, leaving us with a sense that a sea change had occurred in man's view of his place in the world, so a fundamental change occurred in the interpretation of Darwinian evolution. The responses to Darwin before this pause seem distinctly dated to us now. When Hardy speaks in 1895 of children's "coming universal wish not to live," and we see children around us now as vibrantly alive as ever, we are perplexed and aware that some factor must have been overlooked in the first wave of response to Darwinism. Today we hear philosophers telling us that "evolutionary metaphysics is dead" and ". . . evolutionary philosophy is out of fashion."[48] Why?

Evolutionary science itself produced at least partial answers to such questions. Darwin, perhaps at a loss for a more precise solution, had located the source of evolutionary change in *chance* variations. On these the process of natural selection could then capitalize, new forms of life could evolve. But was it really pure accident which brought about the productive variations? Gregor Mendel's work— "published" in 1866 but rediscovered only in 1900—suggested no. Darwin's theory of chance variation proved to be less a solution to the problem of evolutionary change than an incentive to the new science of genetics, which sought to reveal the nature and the cause of mutations. "Evolutionary metaphysics" has waned, in part, because

---

[48] Quotations from Hardy, *Jude the Obscure*, Pt. VI, Chap. 2; J. H. Kultgen, "Biological Evolution and American Metaphysics," in *The Impact of Darwinian Thought*, p. 84; and James Street Fulton, "Philosophical Adventures," p. 1.

the center of scientific inquiry has shifted from the metaphysical to the specific, from speculations on chance mutation to a probing of the evidence of genetics.

Much more important to the literary culture of these years was the shift of primary interest from the Darwinian theory in general to a particular, almost "passing" element in that theory—*chance*. Here the responses to Darwinism were linked with the findings of other sciences which were revealing an uncertain, relativistic world. More and more the mind fixed upon the element of chance, which, after all, lay logically at the root of all evolution in Darwinian terms. In Darwin's deterministic cosmos, changes somehow did occur, but seemingly without cause and at random. Man could only choose from the changes flung in his path. He and nature might select what variations were to survive, but the forces that caused the variations themselves were forever beyond his reach. As far as man could tell, the prime movers of evolutionary development lay in the realm of "crass casualty," coincidence, and random death. In that world of chance and chaos the imaginations of such poets as Hardy and Housman were forced to find their way.

By this very preoccupation with chance, chance itself came to outweigh determinism. What matters in man's world is not inevitability, but flux. All truths of ethics, history, and experience become relative. In place of man's age-long search for the truth, read now his shrewd dodge to survive by native wit; for abstract ideas, read pragmatism; for "the best that is known and thought in the world" and for seeing "things as they really are,"[49] read

---

[49] Quotations from Matthew Arnold, "The Function of Criticism at the Present Time" and "Hebraism and Hellenism," in *Culture*

"learn by doing." Indeed John Dewey claimed it as Darwin's great achievement that he first laid "hands upon the sacred ark of absolute permanency, . . . [and] introduced a mode of thinking that in the end was bound to transform the logic of knowledge, and hence the treatment of morals, politics, and religion."[50] The challenge of Darwinism here becomes a demand, not for capitulation to a predetermined world, but for learning somehow, gropingly, to survive in a wilderness of chance and change.

Just as we found in our general view of the challenge posed to the imagination of this period, so a Darwinian world of chance and flux had its direct effect on man's view of the human faculty of cognition. Man's mind ceases to be an instrument of logic for the perception of truth; rather, "like fur or fang, swiftness or ferocity, or the opposable thumb . . . ,"[51] it is one more earthbound organ evolved in the struggle for survival, to enable us to adapt to the world in which we live but can never clearly know. Our minds reach out but not to fixed certainties; we merely project blind guesses and follow the ones that seem to work best. Such a conception leads us back again to what Professor Buckley wisely calls "the revolt from reason" at the turn of the century. Many retreated from scientific inquiry out of horror at the cosmology it revealed; the later phase of Darwinian influence suggested that, to

---

and Anarchy (1869), Chap. 4. See also Stow Persons, "Darwinism and American Culture," *The Impact of Darwinian Thought*, p. 8.

[50] John Dewey, "The Influence of Darwinism on Philosophy" (1909), in *The Influence of Darwin on Philosophy* (New York, 1910), pp. 1-2. For a full study of Darwin's influence on pragmatism, see Philip P. Wiener, *Evolution and the Founders of Pragmatism* (Cambridge, Mass.: Harvard University Press, 1949).

[51] Fulton, "Philosophical Adventures," p. 13.

our evolving species, the reasoning faculty was at best a candle to help us to stumble less, and, in our blindness, to survive a little more securely.[52] This second phase was hardly less forbidding than the first, and, along with Rainer Maria Rilke, we are left with the stark question, "How is it possible to live, when the very elements of this life are wholly incomprehensible to us?"[53]

Today, with the hindsight of half a century, we can see that this altered view of man's cognition has a brighter aspect. It releases the mind and the imagination from the clutch of determinism; it frees man's imagination to create a world in its own best image, to project and to live by what Frank Kermode has so brilliantly defined for us as the "romantic image." Some imaginations bred in this period—Yeats and Joyce come first to mind—proved perceptive enough and tough enough to see what triumphs now lay open to the poet and the artist. Their prescience is confirmed in the thinking of scientists themselves in more recent years. The speculative reason, says Alfred North Whitehead, "is the special embodiment in us of the disciplined counter-agency which saves the world. . . . One main law which underlies modern progress is that, ex-

---

[52] A nice instance of the overlapping of these two views of man's plight in the world of the new science is related by Henry Salt, who records that, on the same day, he received one letter from Clarence Darrow "informing him that cause and effect determine the conduct of man as surely as law brings the ebb and flow of the tide," and another from "Graham Wallas declaring that Saint Einstein had knocked cause and effect into a cocked hat . . . ." Stephen Winsten, *Salt and His Circle* (London: Hutchinson, 1951), p. 169.

[53] Letter to Lotte Hepner, November 8, 1915, in Rilke, *Briefe* (2 vols., Wiesbaden: Insel-Verlag, 1950), II, 52 (trans. mine).

cept for the rarest accidents of chance, thought *precedes* observation [italics mine]."[54]

But to most men writing between 1880 and 1914 the prospect was less happy, and the spectacle of an impercipient mind groping in a world of darkness and flux was scarcely more bearable than that of a mind held fast in the clutch of materialistic circumstance. Haeckel brought few rays of hope to the human heart, but he thought he *knew* the nature of the world he lived in—and surely his shade would tell us *he knew* he knew the truth. The new view lacked this confidence of knowledge. To touch again on the perspective of Professor Houghton's study: "The Victorians were certain that truth existed and the mind could discover it"; "Doubt never reached the point of positive or terminal skepticism."[55] In the last phase of the challenge of the years between 1880 and 1914, doubt did reach that point.

In the impact of this two-phase challenge we can begin to see the source of the moods of malaise and pessimism which pervaded the culture of this period. First the scientist claimed that the scientific method was "the sole gateway to the whole region of knowledge." The imagination responded, "If Rationalism be the truth, then all literature

[54] *Function of Reason,* Chap. 1. This is a curious parallel to Oscar Wilde's view ("The Decay of Lying," in *Intentions* [1891]) that Nature imitates Art. See also Pearson, *Grammar of Science,* p. 37; and cf. a contemporary scientist's view: "The formulation of . . . postulates of new models is an act of creation and is subject to no limitations of method" (Marshall Walker, *The Nature of Scientific Thought* [Englewood Cliffs: Prentice-Hall, 1963], p. 5).

[55] *Victorian Frame of Mind,* pp. 18, 13.

is simply lunacy, and all the world of arts must go into the region of mania." Then the scientific world began to lose its seemingly fixed bearings, and to move farther away from the reach of man's intelligence; the scientific world has become a world where "all melts under our feet." "I *cannot* put faith in the light you hold to me," writes George Gissing to his sister Margaret in 1883; "it appears to me an artificial reflection of man's hopes." Sensitive, thinking, aspiring man acutely feels his loss and isolation, "each mind keeping as a solitary prisoner its own dream of a world."[56]

Conrad saw it as an age "in which we are camped like bewildered travellers in a garish, unrestful hotel."[57] To Edith Sitwell the age trod "a thin matchboard flooring spread over a shallow hell," and was able to escape the pit only by dancing a perpetual cancan.[58] In religious thought an ominous spread of secularism and disbelief continued. "God hath died," spake Zarathustra, and the theme reverberates through the *fin de siècle*. "Religion is done for—any sort of religion"; we are "dying slowly and surely of Unbelief—and there can be no deadlier dis-

[56] The quotations are from Pearson, *Grammar of Science*, pp. 29-30; Arthur Machen, *Hieroglyphics* (London, 1902), Chap. 6; Pater, "Conclusion," *Renaissance*; Korg, *George Gissing*, p. 57; and Pater, "Conclusion," *Renaissance*.

[57] Joseph Conrad, *Victory* (1915), Pt. I, Chap. 1 (New York: Doubleday, Page, 1915), p. 3.

[58] Quoted from Sitwell, in Routh, *English Literature and Ideas in the Twentieth Century*, p. 179. The view is curiously forecast in William Hale White's *Mark Rutherford's Deliverance* (1885): "Our civilization is nothing but a thin film or crust lying over a volcanic pit" (quoted in Houghton, *Victorian Frame of Mind*, p. 58).

ease."[59] With the collapse of known faiths came an impulsive search for new ones, and a desire to learn "in many shrines . . . to worship the Divinity which is revealed entirely at none."[60] In 1875 the Theosophical Society was founded and Mary Baker Eddy's *Science and Health* provided the textbook for Christian Science; in 1878 the Salvation Army was founded, the Society for Psychical Research in 1882, the Ethical Culture Society in 1888 (the American Society had been founded in 1876)—the list could go on to include Esoteric Buddhists, Hermetic societies, and the rest.

In literature, too, the hectic search was on, for a new abode, "a new habitation for the imagination of men," "for thoughts woven into our subjective life, but which refuse to be mechanically defined."[61] Responses to the

[59] Friedrich Nietzsche, *Thus Spake Zarathustra* (first published, 1892; trans. Alexander Tille, London, 1896), Pt. IV, "Of Higher Man," Sect. 2; Arnold Bennett to H. G. Wells, April 18, 1905, in Harris Wildon, ed., *Arnold Bennett and H. G. Wells* (Urbana: University of Illinois Press, 1960), p. 119; and Edward Carpenter, *Towards Democracy: Complete Edition in Four Parts* (London, 1905), Pt. II, "York Minister."

For scholarly accounts of the predicament of religion in the period, see L. E. Elliott-Binns, *English Thought, 1860-1900: The Theological Aspect* (London: Longmans, Green, 1956), passim; R.C.K. Ensor, *England, 1870-1914* (Oxford: Oxford University Press, 1936), pp. 304-310, 328; Esmé Wingfield-Stratford, *The Victorian Aftermath* (New York: William Morrow, 1934), pp. 119-129.

[60] Selwyn Image, "On Catholicity of Taste," *Hobby Horse*, No. 3 (July 1886), p. 93. In theology there is a marked increase of interest in comparative religion (see Elliott-Binns, *English Thought*, Chap. 9) and in varieties of religious experience; see William James' Gifford Lectures on that subject in 1901-1902.

[61] Quotations from John Davidson, "Windsor Great Park,"

central challenge posed to the culture of this age took diverse directions. In Part II, I will attempt to pursue and to clarify these responses in three modes—as they were evoked in the emotions, in the mind, and in the imagination.

Glasgow Herald, March 2, 1907, p. 11 (see also John Davidson, *The Theatrocrat: A Tragic Play of Church and Stage* [London, 1905], p. 34); and John Tyndall, "Science and Man," in *Fragments*, II, 360, where he ascribes to the poet the task of finding this habitation.

PART II: RESPONSE IN THREE MODES

CHAPTER 3

Responses of the Heart

By responses of the heart I mean those responses which are directly and primarily emotional, not engaged with or dependent upon the intellectual structure or the "second thoughts" of a philosophical system. Such limitations might seem to leave us with nothing to do in this mode but to recite from the literary records the series of emotional reactions to the challenge of the turn of the century. But in fact the responses of the heart show distinct patterns and considerable variety.

Much the most prevalent response, virtually the ground-note of sensitive cultural life of this time, was the mood of pessimism. No one writing in this generation escaped the feeling that man's image of his condition had been severely denigrated, and that he was confronted with a "new despair and sadness of the world." Almost all felt the onslaught of despair directly in their own lives, felt themselves members of a

> . . . miserable race! Too weak to bear,
> Too sad for mirth, too sceptical for prayer!
> Surely in you the Scripture is fulfilled,
> To bid the mountains cover your despair![1]

Arthur Symons has the message spoken by King Solomon, wisest of men:

[1] John Davidson, "Mr. Gosse's Poems," *Illustrated London News* (January 19, 1895), p. 87; and H. D. Traill, "The Age of Despair," *Time: A Monthly Miscellany*, I (May 1870), 152.

There is one secret unto all:
Though life be fair or life forlorn,
Though men bow down to thee or scorn,
Howe'er fate fill the interval,
'Tis better not to have been born.[2]

One cannot read long in the literature of this period without catching this accent of sadness and sensing from what varied points of the compass the note is heard. From the avowed agnostic, Leslie Stephen, in 1876: "There is a deep sadness in the world. Turn and twist the thought as you may, there is no escape. Optimism would be soothing if it were possible; in fact, it is impossible, and therefore a constant mockery." From Walter Pater's *Marius* (1885): "There is a certain grief in things as they are, in man as he has come to be, as he certainly is, . . . some inexplicable shortcoming, or misadventure, on the part of nature itself." From Francis Adams' *Child of the Age* (1894): *"No; this world is not much of a place to be happy in!"* From Grant Allen's *The Woman Who Did* (1895): "Blank pessimism is the one creed possible for all save fools. To hold any other is to curl yourself up selfishly in your own easy chair." Has any other culture, in its cosmic view of things, found so few grounds for gladness, "so little cause for carolings"?[3]

[2] "The Lover of the Queen of Sheba," *Dome*, V (November 1899), 10. Cf. John Davidson, *Diabolus Amans* (Glasgow, 1885), p. 31:
"Nathless, in the last 'amen'
Who'd begin the feast again?"

[3] Quotations from Stephen, "An Agnostic's Apology," *Fortnightly Review*, XIX, NS (June 1, 1876), 857; Pater, *Marius the Epicurean*, Chap. 25; *A Child of the Age*, Chap. 3, Sect. 1; *The Woman Who Did* (London, 1895), Chap. 13; and Thomas Hardy, "The Darkling Thrush" (1900).

Such notes reveal the disillusionment which lurked at the heart of imaginative life at the turn of the century. Was it tragedy? Was Yeats right in calling his comrades of the 1890s the *tragic* generation? Certainly it was not in the classical sense of the term, not by the standards of Greek tragedy in which man fell because, knowingly or unwittingly, he had violated a higher truth, a cosmic moral scheme, which with fuller courage or vision he might have known and obeyed. For the *fin de siècle* there was no moral scheme to be violated; the new despair arose from a world which gave no room for idealism, illusion, or morality whatever. Hardy may define tragedy as exhibiting "a state of things in the life of an individual which unavoidably causes some natural aim or desire of his to end in a catastrophe when carried out." But this is closer to pathos than to tragedy; it is a catastrophe which no faculty of man and no purpose in the scheme of things could have foreseen or forestalled. Man is helpless to comprehend or to combat it. It is "the crime of existence itself," as Schopenhauer, translated into English at last in 1883, was telling the *fin-de-siècle* generation. Man goes to his doom fully and solely as the pawn of a world which does not want him; he cannot help it.[4]

Whether the pessimism of late-century literature informs tragedy, pathos, or the new mode which Professor Murray Krieger calls "the tragic vision,"[5] its sources are

[4] Quotations from Hardy's diaries, November 21-22, 1885, in Florence Emily Hardy, ed., *The Early Life of Thomas Hardy, 1840-91* (New York: Macmillan, 1928), p. 230; and from Arthur Schopenhauer, *The World as Will and Idea*, trans. R. B. Haldane and J. Kemp (1883) (3 vols., London: Routledge and Kegan Paul, 1957), I, 328.

[5] Krieger, *The Tragic Vision* (New York: Holt, Rinehart and

abundantly clear. The new scientific cosmology appeared to deprive man then and in the future of all ground for those purposes and aspirations which, by long tradition or by the very nature of sentient, conscious life, had made life worth living. Pessimism in other times had had other sources; here the source was most specifically the banishment of any conscious controlling purpose from the universe. The death of God had banished hope of any providential directing intelligence. "There being nothing human," wrote Richard Jefferies, "in nature or the universe, and all things being ultra-human and without design, shape, or purpose, I conclude that no deity has anything to do with nature."[6] Mrs. Humphrey Ward's *Robert Elsmere* (1888) was to become the classic record in fiction of spiritual bafflement in the 1880s, and it records the cause as ". . . this perpetual clashing of two estimates of life— the estimate which is the offspring of the scientific spirit, and which is forever making the visible world fairer and more desirable in mortal eyes; and the estimate of Saint Augustine."[7] *Robert Elsmere* was immensely popular and influential; yet one sees at once that the novel, in spite of its date, is the voice of an earlier age than the one we are considering. It accords to science the power of making this world "fairer and more desirable"; and it calls on man "to be very patient," since it may be a generation or

Winston, 1960), considers this mode of vision in ten authors, English, European, and American, all of whom are of the 1880-1914 period or shortly thereafter.

[6] Jefferies, *The Story of My Heart* (London, 1883), Chap. 4.

[7] Bk. I, Chap. ix. On the popularity of *Robert Elsmere*, see Melvin Richter, "T. H. Green and His Audience," *Review of Politics*, XVIII (October 1956), 452-453.

even more before present doubts pass away, and the new era of belief arrives.[8] But to writers at the turn of the century such promise of science and reward for man's patience were permanently gone. A breakdown of confidence in man's freewill and ability to reach truth through reason had banished his hope of shaping or controlling his own destiny. "An irrational Universe which accidentally turns out a few reasoning animals at one corner of it . . . is a Universe which we might well despise if we did not ourselves share its degradation."[9]

From here stemmed the conception that a consciousness thus crippled is not a triumph of life but a disease, a source not of guidance but simply of intensified suffering. It is the world of Thomas Hardy, where pain and affliction strike in direct proportion to the degree of man's conscious aspiration. For Thomas Huxley himself there was "no sadder story than the story of sentient life on this planet." One need not look far to find corroboration of this view of human consciousness in this age. From Dostoevsky: ". . . I am firmly convinced not only that a great deal of consciousness, but that any consciousness is a disease." From John Davidson:

> I hail the hour whene'er, I care not when,
> The race of man may come to be extinct,
> That with the last of *genus homo* too
> May perish this intolerable pain,
> This aching, smarting, bleeding
> consciousness. . . .[10]

[8] See Bk. VI, Chap. xl.

[9] Arthur James Balfour, *Foundations of Belief* (London, 1895), p. 75.

[10] The quotations are from Huxley, in R. J. Campbell, *The New*

The motif is clear in Thomas Hardy (e.g. his poem "The Mother Mourns" [1883]), in Unamuno, and in William Butler Yeats, as when he protests against what philosophy has been to him, "a daily rooter-out of instinct and guiding joy."[11] To be committed to a world of monistic materialism in which (1) there was no room for any lasting and higher significance for man's life whatsoever, and (2) man was granted consciousness to be aware that such was the case—this was a predicament simply synonymous with despair. For, as a grand old contemporary of this generation was to pronounce, looking back on a life spent in rebuilding the confidence of the heart, "Man cannot stand a meaningless life."[12]

From the pain and affliction of adult conscious life came the longing for a retreat to childhood in this period. The Romantics, Wordsworth and Blake especially, had gloried in the childlike vision, though both had looked for a deeper and more satisfying vision in sensitive maturity. A hundred years later the appeal of childhood was to become a longing to cling to the Eden of childhood forever, an avowed wish, with Peter Pan, not to grow up: "I don't want to go to school and learn solemn things. I want always to be a little boy and to have fun." Hardy's Jude

Theology (London, 1907), p. 47; Fyodor Dostoevsky, *Notes from Underground and The Grand Inquisitor*, trans. Ralph E. Matlaw (New York: Dutton, 1960), p. 6; and Davidson, *Diabolus Amans*, p. 99.

[11] In Miguel de Unamuno, *Tragic Sense of Life*, trans. J. E. Crawford Flitch (New York: Dover, 1954), end of Chap. 1. For Yeats, see his journal entry for January 21, 1909, printed in Virginia Moore, *The Unicorn: William Butler Yeats's Search for Reality* (New York: Macmillan, 1954), p. 202.

[12] Carl G. Jung, "Face to Face" interview, BBC London Television, October 22, 1959.

Fawley also yearned to stave off maturity; "he did not want to be a man." For this period childhood was most often seen as the time when life was good. "Indeed," wrote Max Beerbohm, "the modern feeling is that the child can do no wrong."[13] In childhood there is freshness of perception, the world is seen through magic casements, innocence, adventure, fantasy—the world sketched in Kate Greenaway, and written about in Stevenson, Barrie, Kipling, Carroll, Kenneth Grahame, Arthur Ransome, G. A. Henty, and many others. Childhood as viewed by Freud, Salinger, and Golding is something else again—but their day came later.

In terms of critical evaluation, one may say that pessimism in its emotional aspect, the simple felt despair at man's newly described plight, does not provide rich or lasting sustainment to the literary imagination. One cannot sing swan songs forever, one cannot gaze in sorrowing gloom upon the wasteland forever. The cry against life "as a thing to be put up with," the fastening of hands upon the heart—even the brooding on

A heap of broken images, where the sun beats,
And the dead tree gives no shelter, the cricket no relief,
And the dry stone no sound of water

—these things strike poignantly, yet they strike but once.[14]

[13] Quotations from J. M. Barrie, *Peter Pan* (1904), Act V; Hardy, *Jude the Obscure*, Pt. I, Chap. 2; and "A Cloud of Pinafores," in *Works and More* (London, 1899). Cf. Lewis Carroll's preface to the Macmillan edition of *Alice's Adventures Underground* (1886), where the child is seen as one "on whom no shadow of sin . . . has yet fallen."

[14] See Thomas Hardy, *Return of the Native* (1878), Bk. III, Chap. 1; A. E. Housman, "Could Man be Drunk Forever" (1922); and T. S. Eliot, "The Waste Land" (1922), Sect. I, stanza 2.

After that cry—unless, indeed, like God and man's access to truth, man's imagination is also declared dead—the quest must go on, and new ways must be found to keep faith with the poet's vision "to recreate life out of life."[15] I submit that what is lasting and creatively alive in the work of Hardy and A. E. Housman, and to a large extent in that of Gissing, is not the insistent vision of doom, however honest, stoic, and majestic in its way it may be, but rather the artistic craft, subtlety, and imaginative perception with which the pessimistic view of life has been realized in their fiction and poetry.

As a matter of cultural history, it is worth noting the extraordinary spread of Arthur Schopenhauer's influence coincidentally with the impact of pessimism between 1880 and 1914. The question of cultural influence is never a fully soluble one. The degree of influence cannot be precisely measured, and in any case influence involves the needs and special sensitivity of the one influenced quite as much as it does the force or prophetic truth of the one who influences. Any account of pessimism in this particular period must include, for example, Oscar Wilde's own private and inner compulsion always to "want the most tragic," and Gissing's "intuitive fatalism."[16] Nevertheless the spread of Schopenhauer's *Weltanschauung* must indicate a strong measure of influence on the pessimistic mood as it developed in the late nineteenth century. His major work, *Die Welt als Wille und Vorstellung*, ap-

[15] James Joyce, *A Portrait of the Artist as a Young Man* (1916), close of Chap. 4.

[16] Quotations from André Gide, *Oscar Wilde: In Memoriam* . . . trans. Bernard Frechtman (New York: Philosophical Library, 1949), p. 15; and Jacob Korg, *George Gissing: A Critical Biography* (Seattle: University of Washington Press, 1963), p. 145.

peared first in 1819, in the same year as the greatest odes of John Keats, with whose mature view of the world Schopenhauer held so many traits in common. Schopenhauer's early reception in Germany, at the high tide of Hegelian philosophy, was slight enough; it was not until 1853 that his work received serious recognition in England in John Oxenford's "Iconoclasm in German Philosophy," in the April number of the *Westminster Review*. In 1883 *The World as Will and Idea* first appeared in English translation, and its author's name and identity came into currency.[17] It is needless to ask which came first in the crystallization of late-century pessimism, the materialistic monism of science or the philosophy of Schopenhauer. Good cases have been made for the direct influence of Schopenhauer upon Gissing and Conrad.[18] But in general it would seem that the causes for heightened interest in cosmic pessimism probably appeared in their own right on the English scene and were strongly reinforced by the concurrent interest in Schopenhauer.[19] *Why* Schopen-

---

[17] See for example Edgar Jepson, *Memories of an Edwardian and Neo-Georgian* (London: Richards, 1937), especially Chap. 4.

[18] See C. J. Francis, "Gissing and Schopenhauer," *Nineteenth-Century Fiction*, XV (June 1960), 53-63; and Jesse Green, "Diabolism, Pessimism, and Democracy: Notes on Melville and Conrad," *Modern Fiction Studies*, VIII (Autumn 1962), 294-295.

[19] Thomas Hardy, as one instance, had developed the major tenets of his world-view before he became acquainted with Schopenhauer's works; see Ernest Brennecke, Jr., *Thomas Hardy's Universe* (Boston: Small Maynard, 1924), Chap. 1. Pessimism must have had its causes in other areas as well, social, historical, economic; and there may even have been some presiding tide of thought which carried through from the post-Napoleonic, post-romantic disillusionment to the despair of the *fin de siècle*. But if so, that tide lies, for me at least, at what T. S. Eliot once called "a depth at which words and concepts fail us" ("Milton II," in

hauer's work came so pat to the despairing mood of this generation is easy to see. Many of his major themes, as if by prophecy, accorded with the late-century view of the world. Schopenhauer saw the world at the mercy of a blind, overpowering force which he called the Will, and which the feeble human intellect was helpless to shape or affect; he saw human consciousness therefore as caught in endless predetermined conflict and flux, and as the pawn, for all man might ever know, of aimless chance; he felt man's condition, consequently, as one of constant suffering, which greater intelligence made only the more acute; and he found in art one of the few redemptive pursuits left to each of us, as it was to Pope—"To help me thro' this long disease, my life."[20] Even Schopenhauer's recommended withdrawal from life and ascetic renunciation of life are reflected in this period, in Walter Pater's carefully prepared mask against the world, and in Yeats's and Joyce's longing for distance and remove from "whatever is begotten, born, and dies." Schopenhauer pronounced specifically that "the genital organs are, far more than any other external member of the body, subject merely to the will, and not at all to knowledge"—and we recall Edward Carpenter's *Love's Coming of Age*, and its chapters "The Sex-Passion" and "The Intermediate Sex," which seem to reflect Schopenhauer's view, and Shaw's *Back to Methuse-*

On Poetry and Poets [New York: Farrar, Straus and Cudahy, 1957], p. 173).

[20] The themes in Schopenhauer are expressed throughout his *World as Will and Idea*, but those touched on above may be found clearly in the following sections: Bks. I and II; Bks. II and IV; Bks. I and IV; Bk. IV; and Bks. I-IV. The quotation from Pope is from his "Epistle to Dr. Arbuthnot," line 132.

lah (1921), which sees evolution as moving beyond the sex impulse to the impulse of thought.[21] All considered, the powerful appeal of Schopenhauer's entire despairing view of the world to a generation sixty years after his first major pronouncement is the most striking instance of prophecy I know in the cultural life of the nineteenth century.[22]

Pessimism was there, and there was activism. The two are certainly related to a degree. The activist shared the mood expressed in Tennyson's "I myself must mix with action, lest I wither by despair."[23] But the activist response at the end of the century was marked by much greater prevalence and urgency. "Oh, this psychological analysis! It is the curse of the age; it has made Hamlets of us all. We reason and argue, and examine our deeds, instead of going straight on doing, doing, and never doubting what

[21] See Osbert Burdett's "Introduction" to Walter Pater, *Marius the Epicurean* (New York: Dutton, 1934), p. vii; Yeats, "Sailing to Byzantium" (1927); and Schopenhauer, *World as Will and Idea*, I, 425-426.

[22] The influence of Schopenhauer's revisionist disciple Eduard von Hartmann (*Philosophy of the Unconscious* [3 vols., 1st edn. 1860, English trans. London, 1884]) seems to me far less forceful than Schopenhauer's, perhaps owing to von Hartmann's note of ultimate optimism, developed through Hegelianism and modern science. Hartmann does reinforce the commitment to monism at the turn of the century and the awareness of the force of the unconscious in human motivation; and he seems to be present in Hardy's thinking, especially of the *Dynasts* (1904-1908) period; J. O. Bailey, *Thomas Hardy and the Cosmic Mind* (Chapel Hill: University of North Carolina Press, 1956), makes a good case for this influence.

[23] "Locksley Hall," line 98. Cf. Dickens: "Action, in an earnest spirit, is the refuge from gloomy thoughts" (unpublished letter, in Free Library of Philadelphia, to Emily Gotshalk, December 23, 1850).

we do must be right just because we must do it."[24] There is rarely found now any trace of the Carlylean notion that in work there may be a surer way of *knowing* than in the conscious reason, and rarely any evidence of Clough's wished-for confidence that to labor is to pray.[25] The new intensity of the activist is born partly of Darwin and the acceptance of life as struggle, and from this there stems at least the start of a "transvaluation of values" whereby the goal sought virtually ceases to be considered, and the struggle itself becomes everything. "The fight and not the victory remains man's reward," as William Henry Hudson maintained, and by action man "Builds a bulkhead 'twixt Despair and the Edge of Nothing."[26] The activity of the activist may be read variously as the "perpetual 'can-can' " which Edith Sitwell describes, or the resolve to use all of our abilities simply because nature has given them to us, and by using them to increase our lives. "The way to spiritual life," wrote George Meredith, "lies in the complete unfolding of the creature, not in the nipping of his passions. . . . To the flourishing of the spirit, . . . through the healthy exercise of the senses. These are simple tru-

[24] John Davidson and C. J. Wills, *Laura Ruthven's Widowhood* (3 vols., London, 1892), III, 157.

[25] See especially Bks. II and III of Carlyle's *Sartor Resartus*, and Clough's poem, "*Qui Laborat, Orat*."

[26] Quotations from Morley Roberts, *W. H. Hudson: A Portrait* (London: Nash and Grayson, 1924), p. 143; and Rudyard Kipling, "The Supports," poem appended to "On the Gate," in *Debits and Credits* (London: Macmillan, 1926). Miss J.M.S. Tompkins, in her *The Art of Rudyard Kipling* (London: Methuen, 1959), especially in Chap. 7, gives a valuable study of Kipling's sense of the efficacy of work in combatting "the unplumbed blackness" in which man has been placed in this world.

isms." Oscar Wilde's Lord Henry Wotton echoes the thought: "To realise one's nature perfectly—that is what each of us is here for."[27]

Beyond the theme of self-realization there are traces of existentialism in the activist response, in the defiance of Henley's "Invictus," or in Chesterton's faith (which he sets, to be sure, in the Christian tradition) "that the more hopeless is the situation the more hopeful must be the man."[28] Activism at the close of the century could, in each of its aspects, override all systems, faiths, and ultimate principles and, in its impulsive resolve, become an end in itself. Kipling's Tomlinson was turned back from the gates of Heaven and Hell not because he had acted rightly or wrongly, but because he had not acted at all. "'My right!'" cries Kipling's Ortheris, "'My right! I ain't a recruity to go whinin' about my rights to this an' my rights to that, as if I couldn't look after myself. My rights! 'Strewth A'mighty! I'm a man.'"[29]

Further responses of the heart in the literature of this generation fall into a striking dichotomy. The split begins when the premise is accepted that man in his new condition has been cut away from all that is divine and otherworldly, and has been flung back to the world of terrestrial things, brute, physical, material, and that man must make do now, unassisted, with his earth-born nature. The di-

[27] Quotations from Meredith, letter to Mrs. J. B. Gilman, March 16, 1888, *Letters of George Meredith*, ed. by his son (2 vols., New York: Scribner's, 1912), II, 409; and *Dorian Gray,* Chap. 2.

[28] Gilbert K. Chesterton, *Heretics* (London: John Lane, 1914), Chap. 9.

[29] Rudyard Kipling, "His Private Honour" (penultimate paragraph), in *Many Inventions* (1893).

chotomy of response becomes clear when we ask: What, then, is the quality of this earthbound nature which man now must make do with?

The response to that question was characteristically one of either gladness or cynicism. In accord with the monistic inclination of the time, writers rarely exhibited both responses simultaneously. Man in his earthly essence is either good—sensitive, sympathetic, altruistically concerned for others, linked with the ongoing surge of all life—or he is self-seeking and power-hungry, red in tooth and claw. The division might seem local and adventitious, until we recall the antitheses of Locke and Hobbes, Mandeville and Shaftesbury before, and of Jung and Freud in the years after the 1880-1914 period. It may be that the polarity of viewing man as basically either altruistic or selfish is as timeless in human nature as the ones between Platonist and Aristotelian, or Coleridgean and Benthamite.

English literature between 1880 and 1914, at any rate, shows the two lines of response clearly. To take the more cynical line first, there is the egotism born directly of the struggle for survival, the investment of confidence in one's own force and native wit—there being now no other strength on which to rely.

> . . . One must become
> Fanatic—be a wedge—a thunder-bolt,
> To smite a passage through the close-grained world.

So writes John Davidson. This is the imagination which, in an age desperate for certainties, would agree with Freud that "there is nothing we are more certain of than the feeling of our self, our own ego." This is the response that calls Max Stirner into recognition, Ibsen's Brand and

Peer Gynt, and most of all Friedrich Nietzsche, whose works, ushered in by George Egerton, Havelock Ellis, George Bernard Shaw, and others, received their first publication in English from 1896 on. This is the mood of George Moore when he names pity as the "most vile of all vile virtues" and condemns a world that would propose "to interrupt the terrible austere laws of nature which ordain that the weak shall be trampled upon." In this vein Oscar Wilde will woefully confess, after his downfall, that his great failure was that he had doubted himself.[30]

More productive in this type of response is the notion that each man, endowed as he unalterably is with his own peculiar character and characteristics, must take it as his obligation in life and in art to explore and obey and assert that character to the fullest. Emerson had sounded the call to self-reliance decades before, and the influence of Emerson and Whitman certainly grew in the late century in England. But, strictly, the new self-reliance was not Emerson's. The idea that, owing to some divine scheme, each "eye was placed where one ray should fall, that it might testify of that particular ray" was not there in the late century. The new gospel of self-fulfillment was radically agnostic; it took each man's character simply as it was and

[30] Quotations from Davidson, *Smith: A Tragedy* (Glasgow, 1888), closing lines of Act I; Sigmund Freud, *Civilization and Its Discontents* (1930) (London: Hogarth Press, 1955), Chap. 1; and Moore, *Confessions of a Young Man* (London, 1888), Chap. 8. The reference to Wilde is from André Gide, *The Journals of André Gide*, trans. Justin O'Brien (3 vols., New York: Knopf, 1947-1949), II, 400. On this general crescendo of subjectivism in the late century, see Geoffrey Bruun, *Nineteenth-Century European Civilization, 1815-1914* (New York: Oxford University Press, 1960), pp. 192-193.

asked that it be fully obeyed and faithfully expressed. "There is only one true morality for every man; but every man has not the same true morality." This view quickly colored the *fin-de-siècle* conception of art, which was now to be what Baudelaire had wished it to be, "the distillation and centralization of the ego"; and Edward Carpenter, "character and the statement of Self"; and Henry W. Nevinson, "the perfect utterance of the poet's life and true self."[31] What is missing here is any suggestion of an underlying, preordained, and possibly divine harmony upon which the diversity of egos was to be based.

There was still another widespread response of the disillusioned heart in hedonism. There is no question, I think, that the sources of hedonism, in this period as in others, lay in disillusionment, cynicism, and a reversion to self-centered satisfactions. Hedonism involves abandonment of much that gives sustenance to the human imagination, of the past and the future, of "looking before and after," and concentrates on the evanescent *now*. In our best-known

[31] The quotations are, successively, from Ralph Waldo Emerson, "Self-Reliance" (1841); George Bernard Shaw, *Major Barbara* (1907), Act I (cf. Friedrich Nietzsche, *Thus Spake Zarathustra* [English translation, 1896], Pt. III, "Of the Spirit of Gravity": "This—is *my* way,—where is yours? . . . For *the* way—existeth not!"); Charles Baudelaire, *My Heart Laid Bare and Other Prose Writings*, Peter Quennell, ed. (London: Weidenfield and Nicolson, 1950), p. 175; Carpenter, *My Days and Dreams* (London: Allen and Unwin, 1916), p. 86; and Nevinson, *Changes and Chances* (London: Nisbet, 1923), p. 302, quoting Yeats's lecture, "The Three Kings" (May 29, 1903). Cf. Selwyn Image's suggestion of a literary and artistic journal which ". . . would have no principles and no policy. . . . The editor should have no further care than to see that his writers possess individuality and can express it. . . ." ("Of Criticism and the Critic," *Savoy*, No. 1 [January 1896], p. 143.)

expressions of the creed there is a close association between sensuous pleasure and a vivid sense of transiency:

Let us eat and drink; for tomorrow we shall die.

Gather ye rosebuds while ye may,
Old Time is still a-flying.[32]

So it was in this period of transformation when the hedonistic motif became urgent and frenzied. The erasure of all hope for absolute truths of the spirit or the imagination brought in its wake an intensified concentration on the present, the "eternal Nowness";[33] on the *visible*, on being "one of those *pour qui le monde visible* exists";[34] on direct, immediate impressions, on the data of the senses, and on living "in the concrete."[35] The reader may be tempted—is invited—to pursue the theme of *nowness* as it pervades the late century. One of its shaping influences, Walt Whitman, had insisted:

[32] Quotations from Isaiah, XXII, 13; and Robert Herrick, "To the Virgins to Make Much of Time." Cf. Frederick J. Hoffman, *Freudianism and the Literary Mind* (New York: Grove, 1959), p. 299: Implicit in hedonism "is a pervasive skepticism about the absolute validity of any truth. . . ." "Epicureanism," writes William Barrett in his *Irrational Man* (New York: Doubleday, 1958), p. 163, ". . . is haunted by the images of despair."

[33] The phrase is from Edward Carpenter, *Towards Democracy* (London, 1905), p. 82. For other evidence of the theme, see Pater's *Marius*, pp. 79-80, 84, 85; Max Stirner, *The Ego and His Own*, trans. Steven T. Byington (London: Fifield, 1912), pp. 428, 436; Whitman, "Song of Myself" (Sect. 3), in *Leaves of Grass* (1855); Jefferies, *Story of My Heart* (1883), Chap. 3: "It is eternity now."

[34] Théophile Gautier. See also Rupert Hart-Davis, ed., *The Letters of Wilde* (London: Hart-Davis, 1962), letter to Lord Alfred Douglas, January-March 1897, p. 509; and Moore, *Confessions*, p. 185.

[35] Pater, *Marius*, p. 94.

There was never any more inception than there is now,
Nor any more youth or age than there is now,
And will never be any more perfection than there is
   now,
Nor any more heaven or hell than there is now.

Said Tolstoi in 1903, "There is only one time that is important—Now!" Such expressions are the essence of Omar
Khayyám, who came into immense popularity at the end
of the century. The motifs were implicit in the gospel of
the aesthetes: "While all melts under our feet, we may
well grasp at any exquisite passion, or any contribution
to knowledge that seems by a lifted horizon to set the
spirit free for a moment, strange colours, and curious
odours, or the work of the artist's hands, or the face of
one's friend. . . . With this sense of the splendour of our
experience and of its awful brevity, gathering all we are
into one desperate effort to see and touch, we shall hardly
have time to make theories about the things we see and
touch."[36] This was pronounced in 1868. The full flowering
of the hedonism it foresaw can be seen negatively in Max
Nordau's tirades in 1895: "They fritter away their life in
solitary, unprofitable, aesthetic debauch, and all that their
organs, which are in full regression, are still good for is
enervating enjoyment." Or it can be seen positively, in
Samuel Mathewson Scott's piece, "La Goya," in the *Yellow Book* for July 1896: "After all, physical pleasure is
our real joy. . . . For what is the use of pondering over

[36] The quotations are from Whitman, *Leaves of Grass*, Sect. 3;
Tolstoi, "Three Questions," in *Twenty-three Tales*; and Pater,
"Conclusion," *Renaissance*. For the late-century popularity of the
Rubáiyát, see Thomas Wright, *The Life of Edward Fitzgerald* (2
vols., London, 1904), II, 231-232.

life and of trying to find something in it that is really worth the trouble? We know it is only the drift of years, the desire of youth, the regret of age and then the eternal silence. It is better to let our pulses throb while they can; to give over the wondering and the idealising, and to take such joy of life as our senses give us."[37]

The opposing line of response to man's fall back into the world of brute nature manages to accept that fall with gladness. It reaches with open arms to receive "the magnificent enjoyment of the natural gods, the earth and sun and the fruits thereof," "to be always in company with the sun, and sea, and earth," and to find "the faith that grows in the open air."[38] The principal forerunner here is of course George Meredith. Richard Feverel's night walk in the Rhineland forest is perhaps the most memorable scene of man retrieved and restored by nature in Meredith. Meredith holds balanced faith in blood, brain, and spirit, in a fashion that seems distinctly to predate our period, probably because, as Trevelyan pointed out, his balanced view was due not to proof, but to temperament.[39] For nature seekers of the period—Hudson, Jefferies, Edward Thomas, Carpenter, Henry Salt—the resort to nature was compulsive; one feels recurrently the flight *away from* urban civilization as the primary motive for their flight

[37] Quotations from Nordau, *Degeneration* (New York, 1896), p. 540; and *Yellow Book*, X (July 1896), 106.

[38] The three quotations are from Roberts, *Hudson*, p. 79; Jefferies, *Story of My Heart*, Chap. 7; and Carpenter, *Towards Democracy*, p. 68. Can it be chance that the National Trust was founded (with Ruskin's influence) in 1895, the Boy Scout Movement in 1907, and the youth hostel movement in the years just following?

[39] George M. Trevelyan, *The Poetry and Philosophy of George Meredith* (London, 1907), p. 107.

to nature. The *reasons* for turning back to nature are never far from our consciousness as we read in these writers. From a reach upwards to the divine, they deliberately turn to reach downwards, through the maze of civilized shams to solid ground, "to the Earth itself. . . . This—is it not the eternal precept?—is the first thing: to dig downwards." It is the voice of Whitman heard again:

> And limitless are leaves stiff or drooping in the fields,
> And brown ants in the little wells beneath them,
> And mossy scabs of the worm fence, heap'd
> stones, elder, mullein and poke-weed.[40]

It is the voice of Thoreau. Both Whitman and Thoreau were an inspiration to those impelled toward nature and the simple life at the turn of the century.

To reach out with acceptance to the natural world was not only to reach downward, but also to become reunited with a world of age-long duration, through which man was linked with all history, with pagan worship and myth, even with prehistory. The imagination brooded often, as in Hardy, Gissing, and Hudson, on the timelessness of the life with which man was now united, which

---

[40] Quotations from Carpenter, *Towards Democracy*, p. 28 (cf. Lawrence's letter to Willard Johnson, early autumn, 1922, in Aldous Huxley, ed., *The Letters of D. H. Lawrence* [New York: Viking, 1936], p. 564: "God enters from below."); and "Song of Myself" (Sect. 5), in *Leaves of Grass* (1855). Evidence of Whitman's influence in this period is everywhere apparent, e.g., Stephen Winsten, *Salt and His Circle* (London: Hutchinson, 1951), p. 62; Havelock Ellis, *My Life* (London: Heinemann, 1940), pp. 132, 144, 160; Jepson, *Memoirs of an Edwardian and Neo-Georgian*, p. 36; Ernest Rhys, *Everyman Remembers* (London: Dent, 1931), pp. 128-132; Richard Le Gallienne, *The Romantic '90s* (London: Putnam, 1951), p. 129.

> . . . will go onward the same
> Though Dynasties pass.[41]

It was a reunion, too, with the senses and instincts of the animal kingdom, senses fresher and keener than our own. Perhaps in animal instinct, in the unconscious, there might lie faculties of knowing which are superior to man's weary march of mind. "My great religion," writes D. H. Lawrence in 1913, "is a belief in the blood, the flesh, as being wiser than the intellect. We can go wrong in our minds. But what our blood feels and believes and says, is always true."[42] Most of all, reunion with brute nature, even with Darwin's nature, brought a kinship in which man could rejoice; we are "part and parcel of the great community of living beings, indissolubly connected with them from the lowest to the highest by a thousand ties." A new brotherhood of living things can be born.

> Heart, be young; once more it is the ancient
> joy of earth
> Breathes in thee and flings the wild wings
> sunward to the dome
> To the light where all the children of the
> fire had birth
> Though our hearts and footsteps wander
> far from home.[43]

For those who find altruism, joy, and goodness native

---

[41] Hardy, "In Time of 'The Breaking of Nations'" (1870).

[42] Letter to Ernest Collings, January 17, 1913, in Huxley, ed., *Letters*, p. 96.

[43] Quotations from Richard Jefferies (1895), quoted in Edward Thomas, *Richard Jefferies, His Life and Work* (London, 1909), p. 193; and A. E. (George Russell), "The Joy of Earth," last stanza.

to the human heart, kinship with all living things has a further consequence. One has only to combine it with the earlier motif of the sadness of sentient life in a Darwinian world to arrive at a final dimension of emotional response to the late-century challenge: sympathy with all who suffer. Many writers of the time made the connection clear. Walter Pater: "The capacity for suffering [being] so large a principle in things, . . . the only principle, perhaps, to which we may always safely trust is a ready sympathy with the pain one actually sees." Grant Allen: "Pessimism is sympathy. Optimism is selfishness. . . . The pessimist . . . recognizing the seething mass of misery at his doors gives what he can—his pity, or, where possible, his faint aid, in redressing the crying inequalities and injustices of man or nature."[44] R. J. Campbell: "We seem to be more sensitive to the presence of pain as well as more sympathetic than our fathers were, and this tendency shows itself in a recognition of the solidarity of humanity with the lower creation." The existentialist, somewhat later, can make the same point for us in reverse: "Suffering, and pity which is born of suffering, are what reveal to us the brotherhood of every existing thing and more or less of consciousness."[45] Even the scientist could reach wistfully for an altruistic view of human nature in this period, as did Ernst Haeckel.[46]

[44] Quotations from Pater, *Marius*, p. 244; and Allen, *The Woman Who Did*, Chap. 13.

[45] Campbell, *New Theology*, p. 47 (see also Schopenhauer, *World as Will and Idea*, I, 485); and Unamuno, *Tragic Sense of Life*, Chap. 9, p. 210.

[46] *The Riddle of the Universe* (English trans., New York, 1901), p. 350. See also, in our time, Marshall Walker (*Nature of Scientific Thought* [Englewood Cliffs: Prentice-Hall, 1963], p. 160),

From sympathy with all living things came the theme of kindness to animals which is so manifest in literature of this period. Meredith, in such poems as "Melampus" and "Outer and Inner," had embraced man and all living things, animal and vegetable, within one category of "Earth's design." In Hardy the theme emerges almost too bluntly; any Hardy character's sympathy for animals in pain becomes an infallible indication of his moral worth. Biographical illustrations make the theme evident elsewhere: Shaw's vegetarianism ("A man of my spiritual intensity does not eat corpses")[47] and his opposition to sports involving cruelty to animals; the Antivivisection movement supported by Henry Salt and many others; Hudson's assault on dealers in bird-plumage; and Hardy's letters to the *Times* protesting the use of horses in the front lines in wartime. From sympathy for the suffering of animals the response moves up the scale of being to sympathy for the peasantry. Peasants were envisioned in the literary imagination not only as being enviably less sensitive and less susceptible to suffering than men more civilized—"A good, honest, well-to-do peasant, who knows nothing of politics, must be very nearly happy"[48]—but as

---

who finds it an evidence of man's original sin that, though now an evolved altruist, he tends to revert to egocentricity! Meanwhile we must not forget that, from this same matrix of late-century challenge, from different temperaments, there did spring the arrant egoism of Nietzsche, Davidson (*Testament of a Vivisector*, 1901), and the rest.

[47] Archibald Henderson, *George Bernard Shaw: Man of the Century* (New York: Appleton-Century-Crofts, 1956), p. 777, with recognition of Shaw's debt here to Shelley. Cf. Hudson, *Green Mansions* (1904), Chaps. 8-9; H. G. Wells, *A Modern Utopia* (1905), Chap. 9, Sect. 5.

[48] Moore, *Confessions*, conclusion of Chap. 7. Cf. Henry C. Shel-

having deeper and more elemental roots in the scheme of things. Suppose our whole civilized economy "collapsed and fell in," wrote Edward Carpenter; what then would become of the peasant farmer? He "would go out next morning with his team to his usual work, and scarcely know the difference. *If anything he would decidedly feel more cheerful and hopeful.*"[49] It is a theme familiar to readers of Hardy and of Tolstoi, of Hudson and of Yeats.

From here that theme merges with one of the impulses which played into the socialist movement. As early as 1877 William Kingdon Clifford had declared that "the kingdom of Man is at hand." By 1893 Robert Buchanan was maintaining that "human love and self-respect, human science and verification, human perception of the limitations of knowledge, have done more in half a century to justify God, and prove the goodliness of life, than the doctrine of other-worldliness has done in 1,800 years."[50] It had dawned on man's imagination that if man himself desired a better society in the future, then "man himself . . . must be the creator" of it. Beatrice Webb touches on

---

don, *Unbelief in the Nineteenth Century* (London: Charles Kelly, n.d.), p. 147.

[49] Carpenter, *My Days and Dreams*, pp. 312-313; cf. Helen Thomas, *World Without End* (London: Heinemann, 1931), p. 57; and Yeats, *Per Amica Silentia Lunae* (1918), "Anima Mundi," Sect. 1.

[50] Quotations from Clifford's "Cosmic Emotion," in *Lectures and Essays* (London, 1886), p. 417; and "Is Christianity Played Out?" *Daily Chronicle* (London), January 16, 1893, p. 3. Cf. Frederick Greenwood, "The Gospel of Content," *Yellow Book*, II (July 1894), 25; and Campbell, *New Theology*, p. 255. For the contrary egotistical view, see John Davidson, "Windsor Great Park," *Glasgow Herald*, March 2, 1907, p. 11: "The Socialistic revolution is the final stage of the decadence of Christendom."

the point in her autobiography: "I suggest it was during
the middle decades of the nineteenth century that, in
England, the impulse of self-subordinating service was
transferred, consciously and overtly, from God to man."
Frederick Greenwood states it explicitly in the *Yellow
Book* for July 1894: "It is clear that if we must give up the
Divine scheme of redress as a dream, redress is an obligation returned upon ourselves. All will *not* be well in another world: all must be put right in this world or nowhere and never."[51] Hardy's "A Plaint to Man" (1909-
1910) touches the same theme:

> The fact of life with dependence placed
> On the human Heart's resource alone,
> In brotherhood bonded close and graced
>
> With loving-kindness fully blown,
> And visioned help unsought, unknown.[52]

On these terms, the good and the evil of man's life become not divine, but social, values. For Samuel Butler
the want of money becomes the root of all evil, and equal-

---

[51] These three quotations are drawn from Winsten, *Salt and His
Circle*, p. 186; Webb, *My Apprenticeship* (London: Longmans
Green, 1950), p. 123; and Greenwood, "Gospel of Content," p. 27.

[52] See also George Bernard Shaw, "Economic [Basis of Social-
ism]," in *Fabian Essays*, George Bernard Shaw, ed. (London,
1889), pp. 27-29; and Henry Salt's views, as expressed in Winsten,
Salt and His Circle, pp. 186, 191. That there were premonitory
preparations for this faith of man in his fellow living creatures is
amply indicated in Walter E. Houghton, *Victorian Frame of
Mind* (New Haven: Yale University Press, 1957), pp. 271-272
(where he quotes John Stuart Mill), in the "Introduction" to
J. Hillis Miller, *Disappearance of God: Five Nineteenth-Century
Writers* (Cambridge: Harvard University Press, 1963), and elsewhere.

ly for Bernard Shaw poverty becomes the worst of all crimes.

At this point we must pass to the second area of response to the challenge of this period, the responses of the mind. Socialism itself moved rapidly now toward a rigorously economic and scientific formulation; indeed by the time of Wells' *Modern Utopia* (1905), socialism may be considered to have departed from the domain of literature altogether. But within the creative literature of this period there were articulated intellectual as well as emotional responses. To some extent the philosophical mind was better able to meet the challenge and take the measure of the new cosmology. There is some truth in Horace Walpole's remark that life is a tragedy to those who feel, and a comedy to those who think. We next consider the ways in which the mind of the literary artist sought to cope with despair at the turn of the century.

~~~~~~

CHAPTER 4

Responses of the Mind

The literary artist is not of necessity a philosopher, and this chapter does not intend to make him one. That is one reason why this category of response can afford to be brief. The philosopher, meditating on the relationships between experience and abstraction, seeks a full, coherent way of viewing the world; the literary artist seeks many ends by many means—to give pleasure, to create or reveal aesthetic order in the flux of human experience, to convey the feel of existence and catch its moments of beauty. Nevertheless, the artist in his craft does reflect and reinforce patterns of sequential reasoning, sometimes even of a fullblown philosophy; since man's sensitive experience is inevitably imbued with intellection, the artist can scarcely do otherwise. My aim in this chapter is to detect and select for emphasis those literary motifs of this period which clearly do involve responses of the reasoning intellect.

We may consider first—because it strikes so directly at the heart of Darwinian evolution and because it so notably seems to fail of its purpose—an intellectual response we have touched on before, the attempt to read evolutionary evidence in such a way as to restore human volition and aspiration. Basil Willey has given us our most succinct account of Samuel Butler's assaults on Darwin's theory.[1] Butler starts with the conviction that man *can* in his life-

[1] Basil Willey, *Darwin and Butler: Two Versions of Evolution* (London: Chatto & Windus, 1960).

time acquire characteristics which can then be inherited by the next generation. According to this premise then, each man, in however small degree, can both control and give impetus to the upward surge of the human race. For Samuel Butler the perfection of knowledge was *unconsciousness*. Men's lives progress through a series of continual and conscious struggles over new problems to be solved. As these problems are solved, the solutions are stowed away in that subliminal realm of all acquired answers, the unconscious. Thus men are in touch with that upward surge, that Life Force, which impels all living things. So every man is indeed assisting to cure mankind's blindness and to guide his upward course. The Life Force thus becomes not a power blind and merciless, but a source of exultation. To Shaw's philosopher, the Life Force says: "I have done a thousand wonderful things unconsciously by merely willing to live and following the line of least resistance: now I want to know myself and my destination, and choose my path; so I have made a special brain—a philosopher's brain—to grasp this knowledge for me as the husbandman's hand grasps the plough for me. And this . . . must thou strive to do for me until thou diest, when I will make another brain and another philosopher to carry on the work." The ground is laid for Bergson's *Creative Evolution* (1907) and for his simile of the *élan vital* as bursting like an exploding shell into countless individuals and species.[2]

[2] See George Bernard Shaw, *Man and Superman* (1903), Act III, interlude in Hell; and Henri Bergson, *Creative Evolution* (1907), start of Chap. 2. For Shaw's heavy debt to Butler, see his preface to *Major Barbara* (1906), and Archibald Henderson, *George Bernard Shaw: Man of the Century* (New York: Appleton-Century-Crofts, 1956), pp. 786-787.

The strongest argument in the intellectual reinterpretation of Darwinism was not in fact Butler's—which conceived the Life Force as storing more and more good traits into man's unconscious—but rather on the basis of prizing the *self-consciousness* which man had attained thus far in the evolutionary process. If acquired characteristics could be inherited, man could be called upon to widen the domain of self-consciousness and to partake in "Life's incessant aspiration to higher organization . . . and clearer self-understanding."[3] Somehow or other, self-consciousness *had* emerged as a distinctly new quality in the evolution of life. As Arthur Russel Wallace wrote: "Man, in his brain, had developed a specialized organ whose whole purpose was to enable him to escape specialization. . . . Specialization could be left to his cultural shell, his technology. Armored within that shell, great-brained man was in the process of acquiring a sort of timeless, unchanging body in the midst of faunas and floras still forever evolving and vanishing." The same idea occurs in Shaw's *Back to Methuselah* (1921), where he conceives of men of hundreds of years' longevity, who have thereby been able to "press on to the goal of redemption from the flesh, to the vortex freed from matter, to the whirlpool in pure intelligence that, when the world began, was a whirlpool in pure force." There is even evi-

[3] Shaw, *Man and Superman*, III, interlude in Hell. For the presence of this idea in George Meredith, see George M. Trevelyan, *The Poetry and Philosophy of George Meredith* (London, 1907), pp. 199-200. It is curious to note that Shaw's pronouncements on this theme appear to have influenced twentieth-century mystical thought; see Ray Hauserman, *Answer to the Quest* (Bombay: Bharatrya Vidya Bhavan, 1964), especially Chap. 2, "On Biology and Becoming."

dence of a speculation that death may after all not be inevitable: ". . . if the entire human race were united in their efforts to eliminate causes of decay, death might . . . be altogether eliminated."[4]

Such reasoning and such hopes informed much of the socialist impulse which was so manifest in this period. If man's self-conscious understanding was his one instrument wherewith to reshape his destiny, then he had to fall directly to that task, to turn the Darwinian jungle into a livable world. And quickly too, lest the Life Force scrap *homo sapiens* altogether and try some other instrument to continue its upward surge.[5] These ideas became the premises of much of H. G. Wells' optimism, and, as he says, "never did anyone believe more firmly in the promptitude of progress than I." And: "We who are Citizens of the Future wander about this present scene like passengers on a ship overdue, in plain sight of a port which only some disorder in the chart room, prevents us from entering."[6]

More philosophically, the literary mind could view consciousness as a small but growing faculty in living creation, but one that might steadily grow until it could control the Will itself, moving toward that joyance of the time sung by the Chorus of Pities which concludes Har-

[4] Quotations are from Loren C. Eiseley, "Alfred Russel Wallace," *Scientific American*, CC (February 1959), 84; Shaw, Lilith's speech which concludes the play (Henderson, *George Bernard Shaw*, p. 596, states that it was Weismann who first prompted Shaw to the idea "that death was not a fundamental necessity."); and Jefferies, *Story of My Heart* (1883), Chap. 9.

[5] For this idea in Shaw, see St. John G. Ervine, *Some Impressions of My Elders* (London: Allen and Unwin, 1923), pp. 209-210.

[6] Quotations from Wells, *Experiment in Autobiography* (New York: Macmillan, 1934), pp. 143, 702.

dy's *Dynasts*: "*Consciousness the Will informing, till It fashion all things fair!*"[7] If consciousness could be seen as playing such a new and exalted role in the evolutionary process, perhaps man himself could one day introduce into this process the sympathy, altruism, and sense of purpose which had been so ruthlessly banished by orthodox Darwinism.

The hopeful dreams of man's future through an encompassing and sensitized self-consciousness sought new heights. To Edward Carpenter they brought the notion of still another and higher form of consciousness emerging, cosmic consciousness. Richard Maurice Bucke gave this idea its fullest statement and demonstrated that men of cosmic consciousness, men like Whitman, whom he called "the greatest spiritual force yet produced by the race," were becoming more and more numerous among us.[8] And perhaps beyond all such emergent consciousnesses the path will lead to—God Himself. "The Life Force," Shaw believed, "is God in the act of creating Himself." Leo Tolstoi was baffled by such a statement and said so. Shaw replied simply, "To me God does not yet exist; but there is a creative force constantly struggling to evolve an executive organ of godlike knowledge and power...."[9]

[7] The influence of Eduard von Hartmann is apparent here, though without the Hartmann conclusion that when consciousness gains the upper hand, a collective wish for nonexistence can be made, and the world will collapse back into nothingness. There is a clear recurrence of Hardy's hope in Miguel de Unamuno, *Tragic Sense of Life*, trans. J. E. Crawford Flitch (New York: Dover, 1954), Chap. 10, p. 243.

[8] Bucke, *Cosmic Consciousness* (Philadelphia, 1901); the reference to Whitman is in Pt. III, Sect. 6. See also Carpenter, *Civilization: Its Cause and Cure* (London, 1889).

[9] Quotations from Henderson, *George Bernard Shaw*, p. 581;

Yet steadily, through the 1880-1914 period and after, this hopeful intellectual response to Darwinism was being flatly rejected as wishful thinking. The First World War was hardly a striking example of consciousness "fashioning all things fair." The basic premises of the attempt to inject the human will into the evolutionary process were repeatedly impugned by the scientific mind. No evidence could be found to show that acquired characteristics could be inherited; the new science of genetics in fact provided positive evidence to the contrary. And the notions of a "Life Force" and a self-consciousness dissociated from the laws and energies of a materialistically monist universe simply could not be accommodated within the scientist's world at all. Within the early years of the twentieth century, neo-Lamarckianism, and the optimistic view of evolution to which it had provided hope, was dead.

By far the most prevalent intellectual response of the age, indeed the predominant intellectual attitude in its literature, was a resolve to circumvent, or escape from, the confines of that scientific reasoning faculty which seemed to have sprung a deterministic trap for the mind of man. The only path to truth, said Ernst Haeckel, was "the empirical investigation of facts and the rational study of their consequences."[10] The literary mind in the late century seems to have been determined to display how crippling were the limitations of that only path, and to

---

and Shaw's letter of February 14, 1910, in *ibid.*, p. 589. See the full account of the Tolstoi-Shaw exchange in *ibid.*, pp. 582-591. The idea of a God-in-the-future occurs also in John Davidson, *A Rosary* (London, 1903), p. 191.

[10] *The Riddle of the Universe* (English trans., 1901), p. 337. Cf. Arthur James Balfour, *Foundations of Belief* (London, 1895), pp. 6-7.

discover other faculties of cognition. There is irony in this intellectual response—the scientist in scientific pursuit of the unscientific, the rationalist searching for the irrational. But so it was, and the quests for nonlogical faculties of cognition in this period were many. As early as 1866, E. S. Dallas had observed that "outside consciousness there rolls a vast tide of life, which is, perhaps, even more important to us than the little isle of our thoughts which lies within our ken."[11] At the end of the century the theme was being sounded more and more frequently: life is something which *transcends* the intellect and which is largely inaccessible to empirical inductive reasoning; there are vast areas of truth not known by man.[12] Skepticism of the intellect as man's sole instrument for ascertaining truth accounts for the mood of inconsistency in literature of this period ("Why should I be consistent?" asks Benson's Nadine), and for the marked outcropping of new faiths in the spiritual life of the time.[13]

This response settled down, then, to attack the logical faculty itself, which the scientist maintained was man's sole access to truth. There is a widening conviction in the literature of the time that the reasoning faculty, by its own

[11] *The Gay Science* (2 vols., London, 1866), I, 207.

[12] See, for example, Bergson, *Creative Evolution*, p. 53; William James, *The Will to Believe and Other Essays* . . . (London, 1903), p. 51; and Jefferies, *Story of My Heart*, pp. 158, 172, 202.

[13] Quotation from E. F. Benson's *Dodo the Second* (London: Hodder and Stoughton, 1914), Chap. 1. The theme of inconsistency is yet another mark of affinity with Whitman (and with Emerson), and it affected the contemporary resistance to the marital bond as imposing a pact of consistency on inconsistent human nature (as in Grant Allen's *The Woman Who Did*). For the variety of new religious faiths in this period, see L. E. Elliott-Binns, *English Thought* (London: Longmans, Green, 1956), Chap. 15.

very nature, predetermines the sort of conclusions it can reach. Start by induction from sensed experience, and one is committed to a world of material fact and sensation; start with a search for laws of cause and effect, and one must approach a world in which efforts are more and more completely predetermined by causes; start with a resolve to predict the actions of this world, and one is bound to a past and future of assumed sameness, predictable and without room for spontaneous creativity. On such terms Wilde could conclude that "science can never grapple with the irrational. That is why it has no future before it in this world." Yeats willfully turned away from the intellect as defined by Tyndall and Huxley and Bastien-Lepage (the names run like a chanted curse through his *Autobiography*) and records that: "I thought that whatever of philosophy has been made poetry is alone permanent, and that one should begin to arrange it in some regular order, rejecting nothing as the make-believe of the poets. I thought . . . that if a powerful and benevolent spirit has shaped the destiny of this world, we can better discover that destiny from the words that have gathered up the heart's desire of the world, than from historical records, or from speculation, wherein the heart withers. Since then I have observed dreams and visions very carefully, and am now certain that the imagination has some way of lighting on the truth that the reason has not, and that its commandments, delivered when the body is still and the reason silent, are the most binding we can ever know."[14] There grew a conviction that the scientific

[14] Quotations from Wilde, *An Ideal Husband*, Act I; and Yeats, "The Philosophy of Shelley's Poetry," *Dome*, VII (May-July 1900), 75.

reason did more to *hide* reality than to reveal it, that in its preoccupation with the objective world it could throw no light on the subjective one, which is, after all, where much of men's lives are lived, and that to make its method work, science had adopted its own necessary fictions, of force, matter, lines and space, and had deduced from them a world-view which it then asked men to accept as "real." On one ground or another, skepticism of the empirical inductive intellect increased at the close of the century— one reason, perhaps, for the seeming paralysis of intellectual life in this time. Alfred North Whitehead has called the last twenty years of the century "one of the dullest stages of thought since the time of the First Crusade."[15]

Such aversion from the empirical and inductive intellect followed usually, and quite naturally, a path toward recognition of the faculties of the unconscious. Conrad remarks that "great achievements are accomplished in a blessed, warm mental fog . . ."; John Davidson has his hero Bruce cry:

> Now,
> Right in thy teeth, or in thy toothless chaps,
> I swear, antiquity, first thoughts are best.

D. H. Lawrence's religion of "a belief in the blood" comes again to mind. In Thomas Mann's view, the first third of the twentieth century had "surrendered to admiration of

---

[15] *Science and the Modern World* (New York: Macmillan, 1931), p. 96. Walter E. Houghton, *Victorian Frame of Mind: 1830-1870* (New Haven: Yale University Press, 1957), Chap. 5, gives an account of anti-intellectualism in the earlier Victorian age.

the unconscious, to a glorification of instinct, which it thinks is overdue to life."[16]

One is reminded at once of Sigmund Freud as a major thinker of this period whose work focused on the sub-conscious and unconscious, although it appeared too late to affect English literature of this time directly. In any case one must remember that Freud's study was *of* the unconscious and not conducted *by* unconscious faculties of investigation; his procedure was rigorously clinical. It would be just as wrong to regard Freud as the "discoverer" of the unconscious as to regard Darwin as the "discoverer" of evolution. "The poets and philosophers before me," wrote Freud, "discovered the unconscious. What I discovered was the scientific method by which the unconscious can be studied."[17] There was indeed a long tradition of interest in the unconscious before Freud, especially in the period just before his time. Lancelot Law Whyte's *The Unconscious Before Freud* is the best study I know of that earlier tradition.[18] But aside from the formal students

[16] Quotations from Joseph Conrad, *Victory* (1915), Pt. II, Sect. 3; Davidson, *Bruce* (1886), Act II, Scene i; Lawrence, letter to Ernest Collings, January 17, 1913, in *The Letters of D. H. Lawrence*, ed. Aldous Huxley (New York: Viking, 1936), p. 96; and Thomas Mann, "Presenting Schopenhauer," trans. Mrs. H. T. Lowe-Porter, in *The Living Thoughts of Schopenhauer* (New York: Longmans, Green, 1939), p. 29. Cf. Yeats ("Anima Mundi," Sect. XVIII, in *Per Amica Silentia Lunae*): "Only in rapid and subtle thought, or in faint accents heard in the quiet of the mind, can the thought of the spirit come to us but little changed."

[17] Quoted in Lionel Trilling, "Freud and Literature," in *The Liberal Imagination: Essays on Literature and Society* (New York: Doubleday, 1954), p. 44.

[18] (London: Tavistock, 1962). Whyte (p. 63) finds that the idea of the unconscious was conceivable around 1700, topical around 1800, and effective around 1900. See also Frederick J. Hoffman,

of the unconscious whom Whyte considers, many literary figures had already suspected that the sources of truth and belief lay primarily beneath the level of consciousness. Tennyson, Dickens, and Dostoevsky are examples (though the list could go on and on) of authors for whom emotion and intuition take on theological associations. Most of all in the English tradition one thinks of Edmund Burke ("Men often act right from their feelings who afterwards reason but ill on them from principle") and Thomas Carlyle (". . . all that we do springs out of Mystery, Spirit, invisible Force").[19] In the psychologies of Burke and Carlyle, man's conscious life is like the top of an iceberg, dominated and directed by the tug of currents which move below. Against such a background, and especially in view of the upsurge of interest in the unconscious in the late nineteenth century, Sigmund Freud seems less the discoverer of subliminal motivation than the master analyst of it, the culminating spokesman whom this new fascination with the unconscious was bound to produce.

From here on our quest for the responses of the mind in literature of this period (and now we must take *mind* in a wider sense, including its accretion of newly suspected faculties of cognition) becomes a problem of detecting the major ways in which this literature sought to tap the sources of knowledge which lay beneath consciousness.

Freudianism and the Literary Mind (New York: Grove, 1959), Chap. 10.

The large role assigned to the unconscious by Schopenhauer was another reason for his widespread appeal in the late nineteenth and early twentieth centuries.

[19] Quotations from Burke, *On the Sublime and Beautiful* (1757), Pt. I, Sect. 19; and Carlyle, *Sartor Resartus* (1833-1834), Bk. II, Chap. 8.

The psychologist was finding his own means of access to the unconscious through hypnotism, free association, and interpretation of dreams. For the literary mind the principal means of access were two—psychical research and the new influences of oriental religions.

There are psychologists today who watch studies in psychical research with interest; they are prepared to wait and see the evidence confirmed and a theory advanced to explain it. But few would credit now, without some immersement in the literature of the 1880-1914 period, the way in which spiritualism was avidly taken up by many of that generation. The Society for Psychical Research was founded in 1882, "as a sort of weather-bureau for accumulating reports of such meteoric phenomena as apparitions,"[20] and its findings were looked to with hope by scientist, artist, and theologian alike. Wallace and Oliver Lodge were convinced spiritualists; Jefferies, Hudson, and Laurence Housman had strong faith in telepathy. And it was through his interest in psychical research that Yeats was able to break away from the rationalist influence of his father.[21] ("Magic," wrote Frank Kermode, "came, in an age of science, to the defence of poetry.") For Laurence Oliphant the newfound forces of the unseen helped open the way to a "scientific religion." Many looked to psychical research as a means to break at last through the closing ring of materialistic determinism. For Netta Sy-

[20] William James, *The Will to Believe*, pp. 304-305.
[21] For Yeats's studies in psychical research, see "Reveries over Childhood and Youth," in William Butler Yeats, *The Autobiography of William Butler Yeats* (New York: Doubleday, 1958), Sect. 25.

rett it was the most important subject for mankind to study, "the only hope for a demented world."[22]

Unfortunately, such a hope carried death at its heart. Not only did spiritualism fail to gather substantial and convincing supporting evidence as the years went by, but also it would seem that the very nature of the quest was self-contradictory. To seek to prove by scientific inquiry the existence of a force or forces which are radically immaterial and unpredictable is to invite both bewilderment and frustration. The fact that so many of this generation clung to this "hope" so desperately for so long becomes one more revelation of its despairing need for a faith.

Closely allied to the interest in psychical research in this period was a widespread fascination with the occult wisdom and the mysticism of the orient. Madame Blavatsky was the most significant catalyst of this interest. She lived in London from 1877 until her death there in 1891. Her Theosophical Society was founded in America in 1875, and there are signs of her influence in England from the early 1880s onward. A note of discord was struck in 1885 when, after formal investigation, the Society for Psychical Research denounced her as "one of the most accom-

[22] Quotations from Kermode, *Romantic Image* (New York: Chilmark, 1961), p. 110; Oliphant, *Scientific Religion* (London, 1888); and Syrett, *The Sheltering Tree* (London: Geoffrey Bles, 1939), p. 280.

Strong voices opposing psychical research as a base delusion were those of John Tyndall and Edward Clodd among scientists and, among religious spokesmen, Cardinal Manning and G. K. Chesterton. Shaw grew gradually more skeptical of the subject and announced thorough disbelief in 1929; see Henderson, *George Bernard Shaw*, p. 80.

plished, ingenious, and interesting impostors of history."[23] But it took more than mere evidence of fraud to destroy this generation's will to believe. Yeats was the literary figure whose ideas were most significantly influenced by Theosophical thought, and for him the inherent value of Madame Blavatsky's philosophy was something quite independent of the miracles, whether true or false, which she performed.[24] Through the secret doctrine of Theosophy man found a way to a wisdom that transcended both the materialism of the scientist and the sectarianism of the cleric.

But the Blavatsky phenomenon must not be taken in isolation or thought of as the only link between this period and the wisdom of the East. Many motifs of the time encouraged an affinity to things oriental. The nature-worship of Hudson and Richard Jefferies, for example, led them in the same direction, toward unity and contentment with all living things, "a Nirvana of indifference to all but the exquisite delight of simply living."[25] Kipling, especially with *Kim* (1901), did a great deal to quicken interest in the East. The interest in oriental wisdom comfortably fitted in with the period's fascination with antiquity, with ancient myths and beliefs that have long

[23] John Symonds, *Madame Blavatsky: Medium and Magician* (London: Odhams, 1959), p. 222.

[24] Richard Ellmann, *Yeats: Man and Masks* (New York: Dutton, 1958), p. 69. Cf. William Barrett, *Irrational Man* (New York: Doubleday, 1962), pp. 55-56: "The Oriental . . . has accepted his existence within a universe that would appear to be meaningless, to the rational Western mind, and has lived with this meaninglessness."

[25] Jefferies' essay, "Marlborough Forest" (1875 or 1876), quoted in Edward Thomas, *Richard Jefferies: His Life and Work* (London, 1909), p. 109.

been a part of man's imagination, with the aversion to the growing complexities of modern civilization, and with the longing for the simplicity of a more primitive life. Even Shaw felt this; he appreciated "the superiority of the oriental discipline of spiritual contemplation over the fever of occidental hustle, efficiency, and unresting pursuit of material gain."[26] Most of all, oriental, and especially Indian, thought seems to offer a way of "knowing" through the agency of the unconscious and of avoiding the dismal conclusions of Western intellection. All these things drew Edward Carpenter to the orient in 1890-1891; he recorded his visit with the *gñani* in Ceylon: "He was in some respects a high type of pre-civilization man. For, like most men of this class in India, he identified himself so closely with the ancient religious tradition that one could almost feel him to be one of the old Vedic race of two thousand or three thousand years back. . . . And here in this man it was of absorbing interest to feel one came in contact with the root-thought of all existence . . . the germinal idea which in one form or another has spread from nation to nation, and become the soul and impulse of religion after religion. . . . After seeing Whitman, the amazing representative of the same spirit in all its voluminous modern unfoldment—seven years before—this visit to the Eastern sage was like going back to the pure lucid intensely transparent source of some mighty and turbulent stream."[27]

The attraction of the literary mind in this period to oriental thought is so pronounced that there are even some

---

[26] Henderson, *George Bernard Shaw*, p. 663.

[27] Carpenter, *My Days and Dreams* (London: Allen and Unwin, 1921), pp. 143-144. Note this further indication of Whitman's appeal in this period and the grounds for it.

instances of Western literature's influencing the East. Mahatma Gandhi wrote to Henry Salt to thank him for his books on Thoreau, which had led Gandhi to his policy of noncooperation; and it seems possible that Shaw's emphatic adherence to the Life Force as a fountain of "wider, deeper, intenser self-consciousness, and clearer self-understanding" has influenced Hindu seers of the present century.[28]

Perhaps there is one further intellectual response to the challenge faced by the literary mind in this period which should be recorded: it did to some extent attempt to come to grips intellectually with despair and with the fact of pessimism itself. This response must be considered with two reservations in mind: (1) the main counterattack against pessimism is more a matter of human resilience and courage than it is of the intellect (and as such it will be treated more fully in the closing chapter), and (2) the major triumph over pessimism—the existentialist triumph—comes somewhat after the period we are considering.

Thomas Hardy provides the clue to the definitely intellectual response to pessimism made by writers during these years: "As to pessimism. My motto is, first correctly diagnose the complaint . . . and ascertain the cause: then set about finding a remedy if one exists." The challenge to the mind became a challenge to comprehend and to see in perspective the main burden of the assault, and then to train the mind and the human sensibility to meet it or to live with it; to accommodate in one's view of the world what Cary's Gulley Jimson was to call "the nevermore

[28] Stephen Winsten, *Salt and His Circle* (London: Hutchinson, 1951), p. 169; Shaw, *Man and Superman* (1903), Act III.

96

feeling."[29] To go this far was to pass far beyond the cheery impercipience of the agnostic, and to avoid at least the fool's gold that waited at the end of the rainbow for Auguste Comte and John Morley, among others. George Gissing, in a remarkably prescient essay of 1882, recognized this and concluded that a forthright acceptance of man's predicament is a greater incentive to courage and initiative than any form of agnostic "optimism." Forthright acceptance triggered Unamuno's triumphant response: "If it is nothingness that awaits us, let us make an injustice of it; let us fight against destiny, even though without hope of victory; let us fight against it quixotically."[30]

From objectivity, acceptance, and perspective, a further response could be gained—the comic vision. Shaw's dictum finds its place here: "You must not permit the tragic significance of life to take hold of you until you have mastered it and turned it into laughter. . . . I want to reach the melting-point in human beings through laughter. I want the people to go away from my plays feeling a little bigger than when they came to them. To have laughed themselves out of littleness." And, finally, direct confrontation with pessimism, and a resolve to know the worst, fell directly in accord with the passion of this age

[29] Quotations from Hardy, diary entry for January 16, 1918, in Florence Emily Hardy, *The Later Years of Thomas Hardy, 1892-1928* (New York: Macmillan, 1930), p. 183; and Joyce Cary, *The Horse's Mouth* (New York: Harper, 1950), Chap. 26.

[30] *Tragic Sense of Life*, p. 268. Gissing's essay, entitled "Hope of Pessimism," is unpublished, and the MS (No. 15 in the Gissing Collection, Carl H. Pforzheimer Library) is not available for study at the present time. Professor Jacob Korg, in his *George Gissing: A Critical Biography* (Seattle: University of Washington Press, 1963), pp. 51-53, gives a summary account of the essay.

for experience and for discovering its identity. Wrote
Nietzsche: "I then ... took sides [with] everything which
gave pain to, and was hard upon me; I thus found the
way again to that brave pessimism which is the antithesis
of all idealistic falsity, and also, as it would appear to me,
the way to myself,—to my task."[31] "We begin to live,"
said Yeats, "when we have conceived life as tragedy."[32]

In such responses man's mind did at least squarely face
the facts of existence as they seemed to be. The neo-He-
gelian philosophers of the time did not appear to do so.
They may have influenced British social and political
thought in this period, but my reading of this literature
precisely confirms Professor Jerome H. Buckley's conclusion that "the average late Victorian ... scarcely suspected
that he might find" in the neo-Hegelians any "reaffirma-
tion of ... values."[33] The manifest success of empirical inductive reasoning had become too powerful to permit

[31] Quotations from Shaw, in Winsten, *Salt and His Circle*, p. 98;
and Friedrich Nietzsche, "Nietzsche Contra Wagner," in Nietzsche, *The Case of Wagner*, trans. Thomas Common (London,
1899), pp. 83-84.

The impulse to accept pessimism, but to fight it on its hopeless
terms, reinforced activist motifs in this period. It led on also to
intensifying artistic creativity, a need to find solace in the beautiful or to give through art an order and a consequence to the
surrounding darkness. But these topics are more fittingly dealt
with among the responses of the imagination in the following
chapter.

[32] "Four Years: 1887-1891," Sect. 21, Bk. I, of *Trembling of the
Veil*, in *Autobiography*.

[33] *Victorian Temper* (New York: Vintage, 1964), p. 199. For
Hegel's influence on British social and political thought in this
period, see for example Melvin Richter's excellent article, "T. H.
Green and His Audience: Liberalism as a Surrogate Faith,"
Review of Politics, XVIII (October 1956), 444-472. Mrs. Ward's
Robert Elsmere, incidentally, was dedicated to Green.

counteraction from idealistic philosophy. In the early part of this century Schopenhauer's philosophy could hardly find a hearing; philosophy was ruled by that "dismal Hegelism, that school of dulness, that centre of misunderstanding and ignorance, that mind-destroying, spurious wisdom."[34] In literature of this period Hegel's voice is rarely heard. Like Hardy's "Darkling Thrush," Hegel's idealism, in the personae of T. H. Green, F. H. Bradley, and the rest, seemed to sing of

> Some blessed Hope, whereof he knew
> And I was unaware.

Man could not escape the darkening facts of reality, nor the deep conviction that he had moved steadily, in a forced march, away from "the old common happiness which nature gives to all her children."[35] There was no choice for the honest mind but to face materialism and its consequent spiritual despair.

These were the means by which the literary mind sought to respond to the challenge of the new cosmology at the turn of the century. Authors turned to various motives according to the responses which they found most convincing and the degree of confidence with which they could accept those motives. For the most part one must conclude that man's confidence in the responses of the mind available to this generation was not great; like the proofs of God addressed to the heart and mind of John Henry Newman, as they gave no effective solace to the winter of desolation at the turn of the century. This fact in turn

[34] Arthur Schopenhauer, *World as Will and Idea* (3 vols.; London: Routledge and Kegan Paul, 1957), III, 436.

[35] See Hudson, *Purple Land*, conclusion of Chap. 21. Cf. Edward Carpenter, *Civilization*, passim.

contributed to the eerie uneasiness and intellectual uncertainty of the culture of the time. "Great thoughts," writes William Gaunt, "great emotions were lacking."[36] There were majestic exceptions—or seeming exceptions—like Yeats and Joyce, Conrad and Lawrence, although even these were able to work out their own metaphysic, or aesthetic, "code of life" only toward the end of this period. Within the years from 1880 to 1914, the intellectual responses to pessimism, as they are reflected in English literature, seem to be the rise and fall of half-beliefs on a sea of unanswerable skepticism.

[36] *Aesthetic Adventure* (London: Jonathan Cape, 1945), p. 216.

CHAPTER 5

Responses of the Imagination

To ask, "What is the imagination?" is to pose a question at least as baffling as Pontius Pilate's; yet, if responses of this mode are to have sufficient definition to be comprehensible, we must stay for an answer. In an age so compelled as this one to think both monistically and cosmologically, any human preoccupation, however subjective, was forced to take stock of the "death of God" and of "the growing murderousness of the world." It was the imagination for the most part that was assigned the roles of projecting man's dreams, of hypothesizing tenable idealistic beliefs, and of creating the artistic work and form that might give sustenance and solace to the aspirations of man's inner life. For most writers of the time the imagination was simply that human faculty which filled these roles, and the opportunities were taken with relief. William Butler Yeats, recalling the years when he first moved to London in the late 1880s, wrote: "I began to pray that my imagination might somehow be rescued from abstraction and become as preoccupied with life as had been the imagination of Chaucer."[1] Selwyn Image was confident that ". . . the function of the imagination is so long a way from being set at naught for us by modern circumstances, that modern circumstances are likely to throw us more

[1] All quotations from Yeats, "Four Years: 1887-1891" in *Trembling of the Veil*, Bk. I, Sects. 21 and 22, in William Butler Yeats, *The Autobiography of William Butler Yeats* (New York: Doubleday, 1958).

and more back upon it: . . . the world of the imagination is as distinct from the intellectual world say, as the intellectual world is from nature[;] . . . it is a world of its own for us with its peculiar laws and joys."[2]

One might assume that a period in which man was so bent on discovering new faculties of perception, belief, and knowing would be a time of productivity for the imagination, and so it was. Yet a contrary force was constantly at work during these years; great confidence that empirical inductive reasoning was in plain fact the sole legitimate faculty of cognition enforced a continuing skepticism of all other faculties. Repeated proclamations that the world of force and matter was the only *real* world left no room for any higher order which might be perceived behind phenomena. For the Romantics such questions had been easier. I. A. Richards has brilliantly explored Coleridge's uncertainty as to whether the reality of Nature *is* there to be perceived by the poet, or whether it is in fact *put* there by the poet.[3] By the end of the century externality seems to have taken over; the empirical facts of life allowed no field of operation for the shaping spirit of man's imagination. The drabness of urban life and cynicism in moral and political life served further to confine the scope of man's imaginative speculations. The quests of the imagination, like those of other faculties of the literary mind at the turn of the century, bear more often than not the mark of frustration in the search for a conception of the world with which man could live in harmony.

[2] "A Lecture on Art," December 1882, *Hobby Horse*, No. 1 (April 1884), pp. 64-65.

[3] *Coleridge on Imagination* (London: K. Paul, Trench, Trubner, 1934), Chap. 7.

The overwhelming desire for imaginative experience was nonetheless abundantly manifest during this period, and evidenced most clearly in its rage for art. Surely there has been no other period in English culture so haunted or so frenzied with longing for aesthetic pleasure as a separate, refined, world-defying element in man's existence. The art-for-art's-sakers were not the only ones who exhibited this frenzy, although their pronouncements have given the dominant tone to many—too many—of the studies of the period. The aesthetic search appears everywhere. It gives the presiding motive to the extraordinarily diverse achievements of William Morris; it transformed printing, bookbinding, illustration and other visual arts; it inspired countless literary and artistic guilds and clubs, new (and ephemeral) journals—the *Hobby Horse* and the *Dome*, the *Yellow Book* and the *Savoy*; it awakened the English sensitivity as it had seldom been before to new movements in art on the Continent (Wagner, Ibsen, the French realists and symbolists) and—paralleling the awakened interest in Eastern religions—to blue china, Nō plays, the *Japonaiserie* of the orient. "There is but one time, the artistic moment," said Oscar Wilde, wearing wide Byronic collar and breeched in velvet, to his audience in New York (1882); "but one law, the law of form; but one land, the land of Beauty. . . ." But it might almost as well have been the voice of one far from the aesthetic school, Richard Jefferies: "I will search the world through for beauty."[4]

[4] Quotations from Wilde, "The English Renaissance of Art," in *The Complete Works of Oscar Wilde* (12 vols., Garden City, N.Y.: Doubleday, Page, 1923), XI, 22; and Jefferies, *The Story of My Heart* (London, 1883), Chap. 5.

Much of the motive for this rage for art was simply frustration, a recoil from the prospect of a deterministic world. Burne-Jones put the matter simply: "The more materialistic Science becomes, the more angels shall I paint."[5] Art became the antithesis and the antagonist of nature and science, of abstraction and intellection. Even if one did not fully believe in the strength of art as an adversary of the world (or share Wilde's confident assertion that all nature simply copies art), still in art there was escape, surcease from pain, and a refuge for wounded souls. "To live through a single day with [an] overpowering consciousness of our real position," thought Arthur Symons, ". . . would drive any man out of his senses." But to this plight art is a solace, and "before all things an escape."[6]

Nevertheless, frustration was not the only cause of the resurgent aestheticism of the late century. Cultural history indicates this much, that the motif of art-for-art's-sake tends to gather strength at those particular moments in history when the bench marks of spiritual belief are obscured. Professor Guérard makes the point intermittently that aestheticism may be expected to thrive in an age when

[5] Quoted in Rita Wellman, *Victoria Royal* (New York: Scribner's, 1939), p. 296.

[6] Symons, *The Symbolist Movement in Literature* (London, 1899), pp. 172, 173. For other expressions of art as antithesis to science, see Arthur Schopenhauer, *World as Will and Idea* (3 vols.; London: Routledge and Kegan Paul, 1957), I, Bk. III; E. S. Dallas, *The Gay Science* (2 vols., London, 1866), I, 312-313; Yeats, *Trembling of the Veil*, Bk. IV, Sect. 1. For art conceived as escape, see Pater, *Marius*, conclusion of Chap. 4; Mark Longaker, *Ernest Dowson* (Philadelphia: University of Pennsylvania Press, 1944), p. 22; Albert Einstein as quoted in Havelock Ellis, *The Dance of Life* (London: Constable, 1923), pp. 299-300.

ideals have collapsed.[7] Aestheticism, based as it is on pleasures of the senses rather than of the mind, again becomes connected with the elements which encouraged hedonism in this period. "If the end of life is after all happiness, and if some of the very finest happiness is to be found in the world of imagination—then to educate and satisfy this imaginative side of us is of importance too.—And this is the function of Art. . . ." Art becomes joined as well to the impulse toward individual self-realization ("there must be . . . about it . . . the impulse of a distinct individuality"), and to the longing for subconscious cognition and expression. "I am strongly inclined," wrote Arthur Machen (and Schopenhauer shared this inclination), "to think that all the quintessence of art is distilled from the subconscious and not from the conscious self."[8]

And yet we are still not at the root of the matter. What we have found thus far could hardly account for the equation drawn almost universally by writers of this time between artist and prophet-priest. The equation is encountered in earlier decades; one recalls Shelley's "heirophants of an unapprehended inspiration," "unacknowledged legislators of the world," and Carlyle's statement in 1831 that "literature is fast becoming all in all to us; our Church, our Senate, our whole Constitution."[9] Professor Houghton

[7] Albert Guérard, *Art for Art's Sake* (New York: Lothrop, Lee and Shepard, 1936); see especially pp. 17, 68-69, and 84.

[8] Quotations from Selwyn Image, "A Lecture on Art," p. 51; Wilde, "English Renaissance of Art," p. 12; and *Hieroglyphics* (London: Unicorn, 1960), p. 120 (cf. p. 130). See also Schopenhauer, *World As Will and Idea*, I, Bk. I, Sect. 12; and John Davidson, "Genius is a thing brute . . . ," from "Urban Snow," *Glasgow Herald* (January 5, 1907), p. 7.

[9] Quotations from Shelley, conclusion of "A Defence of Poetry" (1821); and Thomas Carlyle, "Historic Survey of German Poetry"

takes due account of the poet-as-oracle in earlier Victorian years.[10] But the lay prophet of earlier days became something else toward the end of the century, a being of both mystery and salvation, a priest of the "hieratic beauty and order in the conduct of life," of "eternal imagination, transmuting the daily bread of experience into the radiant body of everlasting life," minister of "an infallible church of poetic tradition."[11] Stephen Dedalus, in *Stephen Hero* and in *A Portrait of the Artist As a Young Man*, casts much of his aesthetic—his search for *integritas, consonantia, claritas*—in terms of St. Thomas Aquinas.[12] And even earlier Yeats had reached his conclusion dogmatically: "The arts are, I believe, about to take upon their shoulders the burdens that have fallen from the shoulders of priests, and to lead us back upon our journey by filling our thoughts with the essences of things, and not with things.

". . . [We must] take upon ourselves the method and the fervor of a priesthood."[13]

(1831), in *Critical and Miscellaneous Essays* (6 vols., London, 1869), III, 324.

[10] Walter E. Houghton, *Victorian Frame of Mind: 1830-1870* (New Haven: Yale University Press, 1957), especially on pp. 101-102, 152-154.

[11] Quotations from Pater, *Marius*, conclusion of Chap. 2; James Joyce, *A Portrait of the Artist As a Young Man* (New York: Viking, 1959), Chap. 5; and Yeats, "Four Years," Sect. 2, *Trembling of the Veil*.

[12] James Joyce, *Stephen Hero*, ed. Theodore Spencer (London: Jonathan Cape, 1944), p. 82; and *A Portrait of the Artist*, Chap. 5.

[13] William Butler Yeats, "The Autumn of the Body" (1898), and "Ireland and the Arts" (1901), in *Essays and Introductions* (New York: Macmillan, 1961), pp. 193, 203. The conception of the artist as priest is found in the work of Dallas, Gosse, Image, Shiel, Le Gallienne, Symons, and many others.

Some of this quest for salvation through art, in this time of crass casualty and flux, comes from the feeling which all great art imparts, of lifting us above what is mundane and ephemeral. "The world of Imagination," wrote Blake, in a passage Yeats was fond of recalling, "is the world of Eternity. . . . This World of Imagination is Infinite and Eternal."[14] This was the aesthetic power of Keats's urn:

> Thou, silent form, dost tease us out of thought
> As doth eternity;

it is the power to catch and fix forever "the Apple-tree, the singing, and the gold," and

> . . . to keep
> Back beauty, keep it, beauty, beauty, beauty, . . . from
> vanishing away.[15]

In the gospel according to Pater, much of art's sustenance lies in its power to link us with eternity, urging us to grasp at whatever "seems by a lifted horizon to set the spirit free for a moment."[16] Pater gets powerful support from Schopenhauer, for whom art is one of the rare gifts of man by which he can find respite from the clutch of sufficient reason and the Will.[17] For E. M. Forster, art "is the one orderly product which our muddling race has produced."[18]

[14] Blake, "A Vision of the Last Judgement," pp. 69-70.

[15] See Galsworthy's short story, "The Apple-Tree"; and Gerard Manley Hopkins, "The Leaden Echo and the Golden Echo." Cf. Machen, ". . . Artifice is of Time, but Art is of Eternity" (*Hieroglyphics*, p. 153).

[16] Pater, "Conclusion," *Renaissance*.

[17] *World As Will and Ideas*, I, Bk. III.

[18] "Art for Art's Sake," in *Two Cheers for Democracy* (New York: Harcourt, Brace, and World, 1951), p. 92.

All of these influences impelled writers in these decades to glorify art, insisting flamboyantly on its independence from all earthly things. They sought to free it from the shackles of ethics and social responsibility which encumbered it in the criticism of Arnold and Ruskin, to free it from all philosophy and even from all purpose. Roger Fry was to insist that the acute power of art derives largely from its demanding no "responsive action" on our part.[19] "Desire," wrote Joyce in 1903, "is the feeling which urges us to go to something and loathing is the feeling which urges us to go from something: and that art is improper which aims at exciting these feelings in us whether by comedy or by tragedy." Still later, Virginia Woolf declaimed against those novels where, "in order to complete them[,] it seems necessary to do something—to join a society, or, more desperately, to write a cheque." In the earlier phase of art's struggle for independence one might expect the cry to be less cautious and more lurid, as it is with Oscar Wilde: "All art is quite useless."[20]

One manifestation of the demand that art be as free as possible from ulterior motives and attributable "meaning" becomes evident in the virtually universal acceptance of music as the form toward which all arts must constantly aspire. Schopenhauer had expressed this judgment, and it

[19] "An Essay in Aesthetics" (1909), in *Vision and Design* (New York: Brentano's, n.d.), pp. 14, 19.

[20] Quotations from Joyce, "Paris Notebook," in *The Critical Writings of James Joyce*, eds. Ellsworth Mason and Richard Ellmann (New York: Viking, 1959), p. 143 (see also *A Portrait of the Artist*, Chap. 5: "The arts which excite [desires] . . . are . . . improper arts."); Woolf, "Mr. Bennett and Mrs. Brown," in *The Captain's Death Bed and Other Essays* (New York: Harcourt, Brace, and World, 1950), p. 105; and Wilde, "Preface" to *Dorian Gray* (1891).

recurs in the work of Pater, Wilde, Yeats, and others. For Conrad music was "the art of arts." "Music," wrote Roger Fry, ". . . supplies the strongest stimulus to the imaginative life, and at the same time has the least power of controlling its direction. . . ."[21] Some of the late century's passion for Wagner may be due to this high regard for music, and may account for Whistler's fondness for labelling some of his paintings "nocturnes."

At the risk of seeming to court the abstruse, and to probe to a level of motivation of which this generation was only sporadically aware, I suggest that the primary incentive for their worship of art lay deeper than any motive we have yet considered. It will be remembered that the first phase of horror at the world which the new science described was a phase of acceptance of the external world of matter as all that really "was." Man was the spectator, the child before the fact; he looked on powerless at a cause-and-effect cosmos which he had never made and could not in the least bit alter. From this predicament stemmed the inner and sublimated conflict between the age-old instinctive demands of man's inner imaginative life and a world "out there" which showed no intention of accommodating them. ("Nature," said Roger Fry, "is heartlessly indifferent to the needs of the imaginative life.") My suggestion is that art and literature recommended themselves powerfully at this time as a means of solving this conflict, or at least finding a new vantage-point from which to see it; in art subjective vision and ob-

[21] Quotations from Conrad, "Preface" (1897) to *The Nigger of the Narcissus*; and Fry, "An Essay in Aesthetics" (1909), in *Vision and Design*, pp. 15-16. See also John Addington Symonds, "Is Music the Type or Measure of All Art?," *Hobby Horse*, No. 10 (April 1888), pp. 42-51.

jective reality could be achieved simultaneously. In his extraordinary prescience Schopenhauer had foretold this peculiar power of art to take cognizance at once of man's subjective and objective experience. Yeats was to look back on the period, and on the work of Aubrey Beardsley in particular, and find it full of honest disillusion but, alas, with "no representation of desire." Havelock Ellis looked back as well and saw on the one hand "realism, or the discovery of things," and, on the other, "idealism, or the creation of things. Art is the embodied harmony of their conflict." But the critical point is put most lucidly, to my knowledge, by I. A. Richards, at the conclusion of his inquiry as to whether Coleridge's imagination assumes that there is a hidden order "out there" in nature, which the human imagination perceives and to which it penetrates, or whether the order is one which man simply projects by his imagination into a chaotic world. Richards concludes convincingly that neither doctrine is the "true" one for Coleridge; the two coalesce, as they should do in a work of art: "It is the privilege of poetry to preserve us from mistaking our notions either for things or for ourselves. Poetry is the completest mode of utterance."[22] I believe that artistic experience at the turn of the century was thought of, however subconsciously, as the one mode of vision which could provide the bridge between subject and object. Surrounded with quests for new faculties and resources in unconscious levels of human experience, the artist could feel sustainment in even this age of despair.

[22] Quotations from Fry, "Essay in Aesthetics," p. 24; Yeats, "The Tragic Generation," Bk. IV, Sect. 16, in *Trembling of the Veil*, in *Autobiography*; Ellis, *Dance of Life*, p. 76; and Richards, *Coleridge on Imagination*, conclusion of Chap. 7.

In a mechanistic world art provided the means for satisfying the subjective demands of man's existence.

But the contention can hardly be left there, as merely a theory, with some slight evidence of hindsight to support it. We must consider two major imaginative responses of the period, both to extend our account of the cultural life of the time and to illustrate the way in which the human imagination did, through art, search for and ultimately discover a means of bringing events of man's inner, subjective life back into the realm of comprehensible experience. The major responses are those of realism and impressionism.

No reader of late nineteenth- and early twentieth-century literature can fail to recognize the strong resurgence of realistic technique in that period. If the N.E.D. may be relied upon, it was Ruskin in 1857 who first applied the term *realism* critically. In Professor George Becker's *Documents of Modern Literary Realism*,[23] five of the six English critical texts on realism are drawn from this thirty-four-year period. Many were the practitioners of the craft of realism: Hardy, Gissing, Moore, Crackanthorpe, Maugham, Whiteing, Blatchford, Allen, and the rest. Edmund Gosse had sufficient cause to complain, as he did early in the '90s, that "We are wholly given up to realism." The forces encouraging realism in this time are not difficult to see; realism closely paralleled "the spirit of scientific inquiry that is bearing our age along."[24]

In a phrase that would fall pleasantly on Tyndall's or

[23] (Princeton: Princeton University Press, 1963.)

[24] Quotations from *Gossip in a Library* (London, 1891), p. 325; and George Moore, *Literature at Nurse, or Circulating Novels* (London, 1885), p. 17.

Huxley's ears, but which drove the editor of the *Hobby Horse* into a fury, realism, whether in science or in art, is an "effort to submit the mind to things." The directive of realism to the literary imagination is to observe clearly and fully, and to record and represent faithfully that which is "actually out there" in the world which we experience. It is to share what Arthur Symons called "the great, conspicuous talent of Zola," the "talent for exteriority."[25]

But realism as a directive for artistic creativity has severe limitations. There is the danger that complete description may lapse into mere *reportage* or that narrative and fictional form may become "a slice of life." More than this, the writer in a realistic tradition must eventually face the question, "What next?" If his purpose is accuracy of representation, how is he to achieve greater accuracy than did his predecessors? Arriving at this crossroad, the realist will be strongly tempted to follow mythological patterns (as did Zola) to lend a governing significance to his work, patterns which, strictly, are not realistic at all.[26] Or, with equal unrealism, he will seek to superimpose a philosophy on his work, as did Hardy, or a socialist pro-

[25] Quotations from Editor's "Preface," *Hobby Horse*, No. 13 (January 1889), p. 101; and Symons, "A Literary Causerie," *Savoy*, No. 3 (July 1896), p. 101.

I assume that a footnote is adequate, for all the spate of literature which the response produced, to observe that the passion for romance in literature of the turn of the century is largely a recoil from drab realism. Far-off lands, in Hudson, Haggard, Stevenson, Graham, and Samuel Mathewson Scott; the Far East in Kipling and W. Carlton Dawe; the new dreams of science in H. G. Wells —all put forth the theme that, urbanized and decrepit as the drab age was, it was time to seek a newer world.

[26] See Becker, "Introduction," *Documents of Modern Realism*, pp. 32-33.

gram, as did Whiteing and Allen, or a plea for humanitarian sympathy and social uplift, as did Morrison and Nevinson.

Yet it is upon purely aesthetic grounds that the "dead-end" nature of realism is felt most acutely and countered most effectively. What *is* the real world the realist experiences, and how complete, how aware, how true is each person's experience of it? The more one ponders such questions, the less certain and the less "objective" one's answers become. Roger Fry, looking retrospectively at this period, puts the matter succinctly: "When once representation had been pushed to this point where further development was impossible, it was inevitable that artists should turn round and question the validity of the fundamental assumption that art aimed at representation; and the moment the question was fairly posed it became clear that the pseudo-scientific assumption that fidelity to appearance was the measure of art had no logical foundation." An early phase of the transition is illustrated in Yeats's account of how artists of the turn of the century might have described their mission: "Science through much ridicule and some persecution has won its right to explore whatever passes before its corporeal eye, and merely because it passes. . . . Literature now demands the same right of exploration of all that passes before the mind's eye, merely because it passes."[27]

This was the period which produced Charles S. Pierce's recommendation of a new form of aesthetic contemplation, that of "Musement," ". . . that of distant castle-building, . . . or . . . of considering some wonder in one of the

[27] Quotations from Fry, "Art and Life" (1917), in *Vision and Design*, p. 7; and Yeats, "The Tragic Generation," Sect. 13.

Universes. . . . Let religious meditation be allowed to grow up spontaneously out of Pure Play. . . ."[28] One senses how this already falls into accord with the newborn search for nonlogical faculties of knowing, and it becomes inevitable that the realist would be asked to give true cognizance to semiconscious, subconscious, and unconscious "reality" as well as to the mere externals. The result was something like Arthur Symons's declaration: "The moods of men! There I find my subject, there the region over which art rules: and whatever has once been a mood of mine, though it has been no more than a ripple on the sea, and had no longer than that ripple's duration, I claim the right to render, if I can, in verse."[29] At this point it is no longer "general truth" toward which the artist strives; rather it is "the very essence of truth—the truth of appearances to the senses, of the visible world to the eyes that see it."[30] It is here that the response of realism begins to become subordinate to what one might regard as a quite disparate response, impressionism.

The point I wish to make, of course, in regard to the immense significance of art to this generation is that art's role was basically to be an outlet for the expression of

[28] "A Neglected Argument for the Reality of God," *Hibbert Journal* (October 1908), pp. 92-93. Cf. Santayana's view that, since "life is not possible without illusion or a judicious life without illusion, life must be evaluated in terms of the ideals that occur to the imagination rather than in terms of the material powers and relations that make life possible" (Willard E. Arnett, "Ultimate Disillusion and Philosophic Truth," *Revue Internationale de Philosophie*, No. 63 (1963), Fasc. 1, p. 6.

[29] "Preface," 2nd edn., *London Nights* (London, 1897).

[30] Symons, "Decadent Movement in Literature," *Harper's New Monthly Magazine*, LXXXVII (November 1893), p. 859.

subjective experience in a world which seemed to have capitulated utterly to "exteriority." The strategies, all of them, of the aesthetic impulse in meeting the late-century challenge are reducible to one demand: psychologically, imaginatively, and aesthetically, they demanded *Lebensraum* for the imagination, for man's insistence on freedom to find or to project terms on which his life in this world could be both possible and significant. The artist and the impressionist questioned the premises of "realism"; they dwelt on phases of human sensibility which were not simply empirical, or in the old sense "sensational." And they went defiantly beyond this to insist, as does the heroine of Shiel's *Shapes in the Fire*, that "matter does not exist, ... there is no such thing. ... To create it is to produce an impression of its reality upon the senses of others."[31] That is to say, the new artists of "realism," aware of the growing chasm between subject and object, became more and more insistent on the role of the aesthetic observer; they became in fact "impressionists." Lena Milman's statement gives us a symptomatic definition: "The most exquisite in life are just those passing emotions, those elusive impressions which it behooves the artist to go seeking, over them so cunningly to cast his net of words or colour as to preserve the rapture of that emotion, that impression, for the delight of mankind for ever."[32] Walter Pater, Francis Adams, and others of the time shared Lena Milman's belief that one's own impressions of passing experience

[31] M. P. Shiel, *Shapes in the Fire* (London, 1896), p. 12. Cf. John Davidson, *The North Wall* (Glasgow, 1885), p. 145: "There is nothing more absurd than reality."

[32] "A Few Notes upon Mr. James," *Yellow Book*, VII (October 1895), 72.

were both more significant and more *actual* than external "reality" itself, even if that reality could ever be known.

And just at this juncture came the major imaginative response, one might even say the major imaginative discovery, of literary culture in the late nineteenth and early twentieth century—symbolism. The florescence of symbolism in English literature in this period parallels what we have seen as a marked change of direction in the challenge of that time—the change from a conception of the mind as helpless observer of a mechanistic world to a view of the human consciousness as lost on a sea of flux and change. For art or any other form of significant communication, effective or affective, to work successfully on these new terms, a new technique of communication was essential, and in this generation symbolism was the most telling new means that was found.

If one regards a word as a *sign*, one posits something of a one-to-one relationship between the item experienced and the word expressing it. The datum of experience is felt to be more or less "comprehended," represented by the word or phrase used to signify it. A language of signs is thus neatly adapted to the needs of the realist writer; close correlation between word and referent is precisely what he needs, and the more accurate the correlation the better. But as men move toward a new view of the world in which the "reality" of experience begins to shift and become relative, and in which human consciousness—now in itself extremely complex—begins to doubt whether it can apprehend or represent "actuality" at all—what happens then? In such a world the word as sign loses much of its validity in communication; a new technique of literary discourse, indeed of any intelligible discourse, must be found. Writers of the period turned with increasing assurance to the use of symbolism.

The peculiar genius of the symbol is that it is able to communicate in a context where a one-to-one correlation between word and referent is not possible, not conceivable —perhaps not even *desirable*. Many have argued so. Carlyle affirms that "in a Symbol there is concealment and yet revelation." Gerard Manley Hopkins remarks that "sometimes one enjoys and admires the very lines one cannot understand, as for instance 'If it were done when 'tis done' sqq., which is all obscure and disputed, though how fine it is everybody sees and nobody disputes." Edmund Wilson makes the same point—although correspondence has not cleared up the apparent opaqueness of this judgment: "The Symbols of the Symbolist School . . . are a sort of disguise for the poet's ideas."[33]

On these terms, the symbol does not denote; it suggests its meaning. It moves in a world of mysteries, vast, indefinite, intangible. It brings many meanings simultaneously into our consciousness, even contradictory meanings. It troubles us with its unconscious significances before its content begins to become consciously clear to us—and indeed it can never become completely so. Professor Seward puts the point neatly: in the literary symbol "the whole is greater than the sum of the parts."[34] To what end does the

[33] Quotations from Carlyle, *Sartor Resartus*, Bk. III, Chap. 3; Hopkins, letter to Robert Bridges, May 13, 1878, in *Poems and Prose of Gerard Manley Hopkins*, ed. W. H. Gardner (Baltimore: Penguin, 1964), p. 178; and Wilson, *Axel's Castle* (New York: Scribner's, 1936), p. 20. See also *The Symbolist Poem*, ed. Edward Engelberg (New York: Dutton, 1967), p. 335.

[34] Barbara Seward, *The Symbolic Rose* (New York: Columbia

symbol function? To satisfy the "new" craving to respond and create nonlogically, for one thing; for another, to tap those levels of the unconscious whose spontaneity the new science had refused to acknowledge. Symbolism opened new doors, too, for the artist's desire to discover and express his own individuality more fully, "to communicate unique personal feelings"—even to the point where the poem might become "so much a private concern of the poet's that it turned out to be incommunicable to the reader."[35] For Yeats symbolism offered the surest means to achieve the purification and independence of art which the age demanded; it brought "a return to the way of our fathers, a casting out of descriptions of nature for the sake of nature, of the moral law for the sake of the moral law, a casting out of all anecdotes and of that brooding over scientific opinion that so often extinguished the central flame of Tennyson, and of that vehemence that would make us do or not do certain things."[36] In each of these ways symbolism offered an escape from the clutch of a mechanistic world, and it achieved *par excellence* the goal so much prized and sought for in art in this generation, that of bringing subjective experience, inner values, and aspirations back into the realm of an intelligible and valid view of human life and its significance. Symbolism,

University Press, 1960), p. 3; cf. D. H. Lawrence, *Selected Literary Criticism*, ed. Anthony Beal (New York: Viking, 1956), p. 157. There are excellent comments on the nature of symbolism in Seward, *Symbolic Rose*, Chap. 1, and Susanne K. Langer, *Philosophy in a New Key* (Cambridge: Harvard University Press, 1942), Chaps. 1 and 2.

[35] The quotations are from Wilson, *Axel's Castle*, pp. 22, 20.

[36] Yeats, "The Symbolism of Poetry," *Dome*, VI (April 1900), 256.

writes Dr. Rollo May, assures "a bridging of the gap between outer existence . . . and inner meaning."[37]

Still, this has not brought us to the major force which resurgent symbolism released in the literary culture of the 1890s and after. The primary discovery of symbolism was that the sense-data presented to us by experience are in fact *symbols*. Susanne Langer gives the best account of the sea-change which this conception brings to man's view of his place in the world: "All at once, the edifice of human knowledge stands before us, not as a vast collection of sense reports, but as a structure of *facts that are symbols* and *laws that are their meanings*."[38] With this view, the human mind moves away from a passive submission of things—observing, recording, deducing—to a new role of initiative and activity. It becomes once more a thing of intuition, imagination, and creation. The fragments of symbol and suggestiveness that impinge upon it, it discovers, will be meaningless until the mind assesses them sensitively, creating from within itself a meaningful order in those phenomena which will give richness and significance to human life. In short, life will be meaningless

[37] May, "The Significance of Symbols," in *Symbolism in Religion and Literature*, ed. Rollo May (New York: George Braziller, 1960), pp. 21-22.

Symbolism may flourish whenever the world of experience is felt to exceed vastly man's ability to "comprehend" it. Hence medieval symbolism, in the presence of a God infinitely beyond man's direct comprehension. Symbolism of the late nineteenth and early twentieth century stems less from the infinity of God's nature than from a conviction that the very world of man's environment had moved manifestly beyond his ken. (Seward, *Symbolic Rose*, Chaps. 1-3, gives a good account of the change.)

[38] *Philosophy in a New Key*, p. 21.

until man imaginatively creates a viable belief from the symbols of his experience and creatively communicates the experience of that belief to others. The reawakening of symbolism appears to me to be, in technique, the most inspired and telling response of the literary imagination in these decades in British literature. It gives a note of prophecy to expressions of the '90s which have too often been read as arty and extravagant. Lionel Johnson wrote in 1891, "A *symboliste* poem is poetical, yet scientific: it is no longer descriptive or sensational, but, in a very real way, spiritual and true." "Life imitates Art far more than Art imitates Life," wrote Oscar Wilde; "it follows . . . that external Nature also imitates Art. . . . Nature has good intentions, of course, but . . . she cannot carry them out."[39] Flamboyant, yes, and extravagantly expressed; but these are venial sins in a pioneer.[40] The point Wilde apparently

[39] Quotations from Johnson, "A Note upon the Practice and Theory of Verse . . . ," *Hobby Horse*, No. 22 (April 1891), p. 65; and Wilde, "The Decay of Lying," in *Intentions* (*Complete Works*, V), pp. 62-63, 7-8. William Gaunt, *Aesthetic Adventure* (London: Jonathan Cape, 1945), p. 117, considers some of Wilde's forerunners in this vein of critical theory. Cf. Roger Fry, "Essay in Aesthetics," p. 15: "It might . . . be that . . . we should rather justify actual life by its relation to the imaginative, justify nature by its likeness to art."

[40] This discussion of symbolism at the turn of the century must make it clear that I entirely disagree with Professor Guérard's contention (*Art for Art's Sake*, p. 73) that "the aim of the Symbolist movement was not to attain but to flee."

We should be aware that while symbolic method in psychology, logic, and mathematics on the one hand ran parallel to symbolism in the arts on the other, the two modes of symbolism are not identical. The center of the difference lies in the scientist's necessary adherence to the predictive validity of his symbols. To make the point quite simply, one might pose, with Roger Fry, "the question of whether a theory that disregarded facts would have equal

wishes to make is one which both man's imagination and his metaphysic may now readily accept as tenable.

When we link this reawakened interest in symbolism with its contemporary theme, the exaltation of antiquity—the pagan world, the sense of everlastingness in landscape and wood, the reborn love of the classics with Gilbert Murray and others, "the Apple-tree, the singing, and the gold" —we have the basis for the final notable response of the literary imagination in this period—its exploitation of myth. The landmarks of revived interest in mythology are well known: Edward B. Tylor's *Primitive Culture* (1871) and Sir James G. Frazer's *The Golden Bough* (1890-1915), to which could be added substantial contributions by Andrew Lang, Grant Allen, and others. Myth and symbol, of course, are not far separated as evocations of subjective and unconscious experience, as techniques of aesthetic discovery. The contribution of myth is to develop and elaborate symbols into story: "Both symbol and myth have the same function psychologically; they are man's way of expressing the quintessence of his experience—his way of seeing his life, his self-image and his relations to the world of his fellow men and of nature—in a total figure which at the same moment carries the *vital meaning* of this experience."[41]

The age was moving steadily toward a confidence that the accrued inner experience of mankind through the centuries did have its *prima-facie* validity. To William Henry Hudson, "for a thing to have a basis in ancient

value for science with one which agreed with facts" ("Art and Science" [1919], in *Vision and Design*, p. 52).
[41] Rollo May, "The Significance of Symbols," in *Symbolism in Religion and Literature*, p. 34.

instinct [was] to have some kind of justification." And so it was with stories and fables which had clung long and persistently to the human imagination. To the Dublin Hermetic Society in the 1880s Yeats proposed "that whatever the great poets had affirmed in their finest moments was the nearest we could come to an authoritative religion, and that their mythology, their spirits of water and wind were but literal truth."[42] Much of the aesthetic strength and artistic achievement of James Joyce, of William Butler Yeats, and of others of the Celtic Renaissance is derived from symbol deeply grounded in myth. Through a rooting of symbol in that deep substratum of inherited unconscious experience variously labeled "the Great Mind of the universe," the "Great Memory," the "infallible church of poetic tradition,"[43] or the "collective unconscious," such artists were able to escape the threatening solipsism of late-century aesthetics, in which, as Professor Charlesworth notes, each sensibility was alone, each mind kept "as a solitary prisoner its own dream of a world."[44]

[42] Quotations from Morley Roberts, *W. H. Hudson: A Portrait* (London: Eveleigh Nash, 1924), p. 227; and Yeats, "Reveries over Childhood and Youth," Sect. 25. From a somewhat earlier period, Professor Houghton adds another support for the new credence in mythology: ". . . When God was dead, the gods and heroes of history or of myth could take his place. . . ." (*Victorian Frame of Mind*, p. 322.) G. K. Chesterton's protest against impressionism and mythology (*Autobiography* [London: Hutchinson, 1937], p. 91: *Heretics* [London: John Lane, 1914], p. 143) would seem to be an index of the datedness of his intellectual position as we see it now.

[43] Quotations from Yeats, as assembled in Seward, *Symbolic Rose*, p. 90.

[44] Barbara Charlesworth, *Dark Passages: The Decadent Consciousness in Victorian Literature* (Madison: University of Wisconsin Press, 1965), Chap. 3; and Pater, "Conclusion," *Renaissance*.

Our considerations of the responses of the heart and mind to the challenge of the new cosmology ended on a note of predominant gloom; the responses of the imagination were able to discover a note of promise. Insofar as the disconcerted culture of these decades did find ways of moving toward firmer ground in the altered world of the twentieth century, the works of the imagination were chiefly those that showed the way.

PART III: APPLICATIONS

CHAPTER 6

The Mask

By this time, unless my reading of this literary period has induced myopia, one can only view its literary work, as Sir Thomas Browne would say, "quincuncially." As we turn now to applications, asking how the thesis of challenge and response can assist us toward a unified view of this literature, the question can easily become, "Which quincunx shall we select for examination?" Shall it be the dance? Certainly this age was newly and deeply absorbed in the dance. Cecil Sharp's work and the English Folk Dance movement, and the craze for ballad and ballet are evidences of that absorption. One may quickly discern how the dance appealed to the new longing for the instinctual, the passionate, and the hedonistic: "The dance is life, animal life, having its own way passionately. . . . It began with the worship of the disturbing deities, the Gods of ecstasy, for whom wantonness and wine, and all things in which energy passes into an ideal excess, were sacred.

". . . These young bodies . . . seem to sum up in themselves the appeal of everything in the world that is passing, and coloured, and to be enjoyed: everything that bids us take no thought for the morrow, and dissolve the will into slumber, and give way luxuriously to the delightful present."[1]

The dance embodied man's desire to escape the divisive-

[1] Arthur Symons, "Ballet, Pantomime, and Poetic Drama," *Dome* (October 1898), I, 65, 66.

ness and sterility of intellection, enabling him almost, as it were, to think with the whole body rather than with the mind alone. Moreover, the dance was a nearly perfect epitome of what the age sought in art. It was almost as highly regarded as music, considered the most perfect of art forms; it had "no words," and hence "less to spoil." It escaped thereby from utility and the clutch of meaning. It brought into harmony those tensions between object and the isolated subject and between fixity and eternal flux which had tormented the imagination. Like Yeats's pern and gyre, or the later vortex of the Vorticists, the dance achieves a stasis of beauty within the flux, it combines "turbulent energy" with "marmorean stillness." In the dance the artist is immersed in the art; substance and medium are one.

> O body swayed to music, O brightening glance,
> How can we know the dancer from the dance?[2]

Little wonder the dance should have become a metaphor of life to this generation, "no mere translation or abstraction from life, but life itself."[3]

[2] Quotations here are all from Yeats: "Prologue" to *The Death of Cuchulain* (1939), in *The Collected Plays of W. B. Yeats* (New York: Macmillan, 1953); "Poetry and Tradition" (1907); and "Among School Children" (1927). Consider also Yeats's dance plays; and see V.L.O. Chittick's brief sketch of the matter in "Yeats the Dancer," *Dalhousie Review*, XXXIX (Autumn 1959), 333-348.

[3] Havelock Ellis, *The Dance of Life* (London: Constable, 1923), p. 60; see also his full discussion of "The Art of Dancing," *ibid.* Cf. Evelyn Sharp, *Unfinished Adventure* (London: John Lane, 1933), p. 294: "This mystic side of the racial dance . . . seems to reflect the whole meaning of life. That life has to go on, that it has to change as it goes on, and that no change is worth anything unless it is based on what is eternal and unchanging in the past—these

Or shall our quincunx be the revival of the "art" of walking? People, needless to say, had walked before. But the appeal of walking in this period was not that of Childe Harold's scaling of mountains where "to him were friends," nor of Wordsworth's vision on Snowdon of the emblem of

> a mind sustained
> By recognitions of transcendent power, . . .
> In soul of more than mortal privilege;

nor the *hinauf am Hohe!* motif which inspired the disciples of Thomas Arnold—

> With frowning foreheads, with lips
> Sternly compressed, we strain on[4]

—and which led Leslie Stephen and his fellow mountaineers to their conquests of the Alps. The romance of the road (and the burgeoning of the "hosteling movement") in the late century takes on a different cast and reflects the changed predicament of man's imaginative life. Therapeutically, walking—a mindless, thought-effacing kind of walking—gave to these years an escape, an anodyne to despair, the "walking alone through crowds"

---

articles of belief, which alone give a meaning to the survival and revival of traditional dance and music in a modern machine-driven world, seem to me also to offer the only solid foundation on which the future of human conduct . . . can be built."

[4] Quotations from Byron, *Childe Harold*, III, 13; Wordsworth, *Prelude*, XIV, ll. 74-75, 77; and Matthew Arnold, "Rugby Chapel" (1867), ll. 105-106. The theme of mountain-climbing as an ascent to an exalted, embracing vision of truth does recur at the turn of the century, for example in Nietzsche's "universe surveyed as from a mountain summit" (*Case of Wagner*, Sect. 1), or the projected "Hill-Top Novels" of Grant Allen.

which was Arthur Symons's temporarily successful defense against madness. Or walking could serve as the image of the endless, dusty, trudging affair which life had become:

> "Heel and toe from dawn to dusk,
> Round the world and home again."

More forcefully, the theme of walking expressed the longing to strike down through the crust of civilization and the pavements of the city to the life of earth. "Men are Antaean," wrote Davidson; "energy streams up from the centre into him that walks the world."[5]

From here the link reaches to neopaganism again—the ancient, endlessly trodden paths of Hardy's Wessex; or, more frequently, to the startling rebellion in this literature against boots, and the accompanying crusade for sandals and freedom of foot. "Socrates and Plato," wrote Richard Jefferies, "Leonidas and Caesar—all the heroes—the gods, too, walked with naked feet or in sandals. They knew nothing of Day and Martin. Their feet were open, free, unrestrained. Look at the feet of the statues—how beautiful! But the feet in those boots—'cabined, cribbed, confined,' distorted, somehow there is something about those boots at which my mind revolts. They are the very

[5] The three quotations are from Symons, in Barbara Charlesworth, *Dark Passages, The Decadent Consciousness in Victorian Literature* (Madison: University of Wisconsin Press, 1965), pp. 117-118; John Davidson, "The Last Journey" (1908) (the experience on which these lines were based dates from November 1906; see John A. Lester, Jr., "Prose-Poetry Transmutation in the Poetry of John Davidson," *MP*, LVI [August 1958], p. 42); and Davidson, "Here Awa', There Awa'," *Outlook* (May 13, 1905), p. 680.

symbols of our dirty macadamized times." Hopkins had pondered a world which

> ... wears man's smudge and shares
> man's smell: the soil
> Is bare now, nor can foot feel, being shod.

Edward Carpenter waged a continuing campaign for the simplification of life—and the wearing of sandals. Kipling's Tommy cries out in maddened frenzy against

> Boots, boots, boots, boots
> Moving up and down again

before him in the march. And Yeats sadly tells the tale of his friend Nettleship, "had up" by the police for walking barefoot in Regent's Park: "I was carrying my boots in my hand and he thought I was a burglar and even when I explained and gave him half-a-crown, he would not let me go till I had promised to put on my boots before I met the next policeman." John Davidson, the most compulsive walker of them all, seems to speak for his age when his Scotsman Sandy cries, "Heaven is to tread unpaven ground."[6]

[6] The five quotations are from Jefferies, *Restless Human Hearts* (1875), as given in Edward Thomas, *Richard Jefferies: His Life and Work* (London, 1909), p. 100; Hopkins, "God's Grandeur" (1877); Kipling, "Boots" (1903); Yeats, "Four Years," Bk. I, Sect. 16, in *Trembling of the Veil*, in William Butler Yeats, *The Autobiography of William Butler Yeats* (New York: Doubleday, 1958) (the passage reminds one of Yeats' fondness, as in "The Grey Rock," for using the free foot as synecdochic representative of the spiritual life; cf. his comment on George Eliot [*Reveries over Childhood and Youth* (1914), Sect. 24, in *Autobiography*]: "She seemed to have a distrust or a distaste for all in life that gives

Still another quincunx could be found in the extraordinary appeal which gems and precious stones had for the imagination of this period. Why must Pater's flame be "gemlike"? Like the dance and the passion for walking, the attractions of gem imagery were strong yet varied, often contradictory in literal implication. To Dorian Gray (as to Huysmans's Des Esseintes before him) precious jewels suggested the sphinxlike romance of their origins and possessed a beauty both vividly sensuous and enduring —a strong appeal to a generation that sensed all was melting beneath its feet. Again, unexpectedly, the Jesuit poet Hopkins is linked with this generation; in Hopkins, too, the longed-for ultimate union of human with Christlike life could be expressed in the imagery of precious stones:

> In a flash, at a trumpet crash,
> I am all at once what Christ is, since he was once
> what I am, and
> This Jack, joke, poor potsherd, patch, matchwood,
> immortal diamond,
> Is immortal diamond.[7]

For Nietzsche gems epitomized his call to tough self-dependence; *"Become hard!"* he writes, like a diamond, to carve your mark upon the world. Davidson's last phase of poetized materialism is strewn with the thoughts and

---

one a springing foot"); and Davidson, "Good-Friday," in *Fleet Street Eclogues* (London, 1893), p. 36.

[7] References are from Wilde, *Dorian Gray*, Chap. 11; J.-K. Huysmans, *A Rebours* (1884), Chap. 4; and Hopkins, "That Nature is a Heraclitean Fire . . ." (1888). Karl Beckson, "Introduction," in *Aesthetics and Decadents of the 1890s* (New York: Vintage, 1966), p. xx, adds further references to support the period's passion for gems and cameos.

images of jewels—"The hardest, most enduring forms of
the matter of which we ourselves consist."[8] For Gautier
and the French Parnassians, and for Walter Pater, the
precious gem was emblematic of those qualities they ad-
mired in a work of art: it brought solace to their fallen
times; it was born of the earth yet refined to a crystalline
fixity, the hardest of substances, yet cut to a form translu-
cent, pure, silent, and shining with a light both of the world
and of its own, a thing of beauty fixed and timeless. The
literary historian, the philosopher, the scientist, the aesthe-
tician—each could account for the appeal precious stones
had for the literary imagination of this period, but each
account, I submit, would be partial and less comprehensive
than the interpretation afforded by an awareness of the
larger crisis which confronted man's imaginative life in

[8] Quotations from Nietzsche, "The Hammer Speaketh," con-
cluding section of "The Twilight of the Idols" (1888) (cf. "The
Dawn of Day" [1886], Bk. V, Sect. 541); and Davidson, "A
Moribund Art," *Westminster Gazette* (December 8, 1906), p. 2.
Davidson elsewhere makes an engaging invitation to drink, in that
in alcohol we imbibe carbon and the heat of the sun: "you are
drinking diamonds" ("Dramatic Weather," *Westminster Gazette*
[September 17, 1904], p. 6).
On gems and carved ivory as images of artistic craftsmanship
in Gautier and the Parnassians, see William Gaunt, *Aesthetic Adventure* (London: Jonathan Cape, 1945), pp. 14-15, and Charlesworth, *Dark Passages*, p. 45. Professor Charlesworth (p. 39) brings
Walter Pater's fondness for the crystal metaphor into revealing
relationship with Coleridge's observation: "Something there must
be to realize the form, something in and by which the *forma in-
formans* reveals itself. . . . An illustrative hint may be taken from
a pure crystal. . . . The crystal is lost in the light which yet it con-
tains, embodies, and gives a shape to." ("On the Principles of
Genial Criticism concerning the Fine Arts" [1814].) Cf. also
Ruskin's aesthetic—and moral—fascination with gems and crystals
in *The Ethics of the Dust* (1866).

these years. These precious jewels appealed not only to the aesthete and the materialist, the immoralist and the creative artist; their properties appeased the common longing which informed this age of flux, uncertainty, and evanescence, for something in life with a permanent and redeeming beauty.

Quincunxes everywhere. Forced to a choice, I shall in these concluding three chapters consider in detail three themes in the literature of the period—the mask, ecstasy, and the will to believe. I have selected these because they strike me as rich and wide-ranging in the literature, because they have not been directly dealt with in this light before, and because, in their various ways, they illustrate the unified, synthesizing sort of interpretation which our challenge-and-response study of this culture can make possible. My hope is that these themes will both clarify and confirm the terms of the underlying crisis which the earlier chapters of this essay have attempted to describe.

One might protest that there is a logical sequence to these three themes which is ignored in the order they follow below; the mask may seem a response of the imagination, the will to believe a response of the mind, and ecstasy a response of the heart. I believe this oversimplifies the case and that in reality each theme springs from the whole cultural predicament which I have attempted to describe. Simple resilience of character and courage to be must be called upon to achieve a willed belief; much intellectual strategy lies behind Yeats' concept of the mask; and so on. I have therefore chosen not to follow a "logical" sequence that would be in part fallacious, but rather to follow what I feel to be a manifest crescendo of these themes as they lend inspiration to the literary artist of this time in his journey through despair.

To understand the prevalence of mask motif and imagery in this literature, we must reflect first on a particular aspect of that underlying crisis and its sundering effect, breaking in two man's imaginative view of his place in the world. Materialistic monism rendered all phenomena *objective*; indeed, it eliminated the *subjective* altogether. In the later years of the period, when renewed emphasis was being put on man's inner life, the groping, rootless world of the subjective still seemed to have lost its relationship with the objective. In both phases the spiritual world was cast away from the material, the world of appearance from the world of "reality"—or was it Sartrean *nothingness* that lay behind what appeared to be "real"? Civilization seemed pitted against brutality, and man seemed "suddenly brought face to face with that other deeper-lying and often semi-barbarous self, which crouches hidden beneath the veneer of civilization and the mask of social habit...."[9] The unconscious broke sharply away from the conscious, and seemed often in conflict with it; intuition, impatient with the confinement and sterility of the intellect, sought its own way. Debates ran on, such as that between Yeats and his father on the relative merits of *character* and *personality*. Character takes the form of the "given" self, the elemental will and stuff of an individual's makeup; per-

[9] Caldwell Lipsett, *Where the Atlantic Meets the Land* (London, 1896), p. 77. The passage is an interesting forecast of Carl Jung's discussion of the "split between the individual and the collective psyche, . . . a veneer of civilization over a dark-skinned brute. . . ." "On the Psychology of the Unconscious," in *Two Essays on Analytical Psychology* (New York: Meridian, 1956), p. 107.

sonality is what one can project and fabricate from what is given—which will you have? Should one lunge forth upon the world, a Nietzschean laughing lion, confident in the strength that has been innately placed within himself? Or, with Max Beerbohm, should one settle down to re-fine and polish, and "cultivate [one's] discrepancies"?[10] Whichever course one decided upon, it is apparent that a schizophrenia of the human sensibility afflicted the age.

A similar dichotomy had beset the literary imagination before, in the Romantics' keen vision of an ideal behind the real, and most poignantly in the tormented vision of Matthew Arnold.[11] But in the decades just before and after the turn of the century, the schizophrenia is evidenced on all sides. Schopenhauer had taught the age that the essence of things is not accessible to our consciousness; all things appear "as in a mask, which allows us merely to assume what is concealed beneath it, but never to know it." The writers of this period correspondingly reveal an emotional turbulence within, overlaid with a deliberate constraint with which to face the world—witness the classicism of Lionel Johnson and A. E. Housman, and "the

[10] Cf. Richard Le Gallienne, "The Dramatic Art of Life," *Yellow Book*, VI (July 1895), 316, who speaks of "creating that finest work of art—a personality; for a personality . . . is not only born, but made." The character *vs.* personality discussion is touched on in Virginia Moore, *The Unicorn: William Butler Yeats' Search for Reality* (New York: Macmillan, 1954), pp. 209-210, and Richard Ellmann, *Yeats: The Man and the Masks* (New York: Dutton, 1958), pp. 72-73.

[11] A very penetrating study of the division between sensibility and outlook in Arnold, and in Tennyson and Browning, is made by E.D.H. Johnson, *The Alien Vision of Victorian Poetry* (Princeton: Princeton University Press, 1952).

enigma of manner" assumed by Walter Pater and by James Joyce after him.[12]

Here the door opens upon the widely pervasive motif of the double in literature of the period. Dostoevsky's double may be there in the background, but on the British scene there are M. P. Shiel's and Arthur Machen's mystery tales and their frequent evocations of a "shadowy companion" who walks unseen beside one through life. "Daily life," wrote E. M. Forster, "whatever it may be really, is practically composed of two lives—the life in time and the life by values—and our conduct reveals a double allegiance."[13] Such a reach of the imagination drew strength from the psychical speculations into the co-existence of an unseen world beyond the seen. Even biographically this was an age of pseudonyms and alter egos, some of which have a mark of authenticity about them. William Sharp's mood and style altered completely when he became Fiona MacLeod.[14] There was Wilde's Dorian

[12] The quotations are from Schopenhauer, *The World as Will and Idea*, Bk. II, Chap. 18; and (regarding Joyce) Ellmann, *Yeats: Man and Masks*, p. 72 (cf. James Joyce, *Stephen Hero*, ed. Theodore Spencer [London: Jonathan Cape, 1944], p. 64).

John Davidson gives an added twist to this theme of the blank unknowability of things, in speaking of "the worshipful IRONY of which we and the world are the mask and domino." ("Irony," *Speaker* [April 8, 1899], p. 398.) For Pater's "screen carefully prepared to protect its deviser from the world," see Osbert Burdett, "Introduction" to Pater, *Marius the Epicurean* (New York: Dutton, 1934), p. vii.

[13] *Aspects of the Novel* (New York: Harcourt, Brace, 1927), p. 49.

[14] There is a striking if enigmatic forecast of the double in Shelley's *Prometheus Unbound*, Act I, ll. 192-193, where Zoroaster meets "his own image in the garden." Poe's story, "William Wil-

Gray, whose mask of youthful beauty faced the world while, locked away from worldly view, his other self, the portrait, exhibited the ugliness and bestiality which lay behind the mask. Surely not the most profound, but possibly the most apparent, exploitation of the double was Robert Louis Stevenson's in "The Strange Case of Dr. Jekyll and Mr. Hyde" (1895). The story, to one reading it now, may seem curiously unsuggestive and unaware of its possibilities. Indeed, Oscar Wilde observed at the time that it "reads dangerously like an experiment out of the *Lancet*"; and Machen saw that "if one escapes for a moment from the atmosphere of the laboratory [in the story] it is only to be confronted by the most obvious vein of moral allegory."[15] But what is to the point here is that Stevenson's stark representation of the double motif had immense appeal to his audience. The motif occurs elsewhere in Stevenson's stories and in stories by Wilde, Kipling, and H. G. Wells, not to mention its earlier sporadic occurrences in Mary Shelley, Bulwer Lytton, and the influential tales of Edgar Allan Poe.[16]

---

son," is another early example of the theme. The double figures importantly in Arthur Machen's *Hieroglyphics* (London: Unicorn, 1960), p. 47: "that strange companion of man, who walks . . . foot to foot with each one of us, and yet his paces are in an unknown world."

[15] Quotations from Wilde, "The Decay of Lying," in *The Complete Works of Oscar Wilde* (12 vols., Garden City, N.Y.: Doubleday, Page, 1923), V, 15; and Machen, *Hieroglyphics*, p. 81. Malcolm Elwin takes the same line (*Old Gods Falling* [London: Collins, 1939], p. 158), in reading "Jekyll and Hyde" as "one of the most shrewd and daring satires on Respectability between Thackeray and Galsworthy."

[16] The best monograph on the double motif remains that of Ralph Tymms, *Doubles in Literary Psychology* (Cambridge

But it is in Joseph Conrad's works that the sense of the double nature of man is most richly and rewardingly conceived. "The Secret Sharer" (1909) is only the most pointed and obvious example of the double in Conrad's work—the captain and Leggatt, "a double captain busy talking in whispers with his other self."[17] Conrad is craftsman enough to see the usefulness of doubling as a method for accent, irony, and tension: thus Marlow in a sense redoubles Conrad, Stein (in *Lord Jim*) is felt as a further doubling of Marlow, Gentleman Brown a doubling of Jim, Winnie Verloc (in *The Secret Agent*) redoubles temperament of Stevie, and so on. But in the substance of Conrad's view of man's fate, the double also has its intensity and ramification. Man, upon encountering an insurmountable plight, has within himself that which will whine and cry pity (like Jim Wait in *The Nigger of the Narcissus*), and that which will stoically stand up to the worst (like Singleton and the crew against the storm in the same book).[18] As Conrad views the human condition, there is within man an impenetrable darkness and in the world chaos and defeat await him. Man at best must project and live by a higher other self, an "ideal conception of one's own personality [which] every man sets up for himself secretly," in a "pitiless wedding with a shadowy ideal of conduct."[19]

In the light of such literary forebears, Freud's dis-

[Eng.]: Bowes and Bowes, 1949), although there is need for a much fuller study.

[17] "The Secret Sharer," Pt. I.

[18] The character of Donkin, of course, serves as the vital link between Wait and Singleton.

[19] Quotations from "The Secret Sharer," Pt. I, and *Lord Jim*, Chap. 45.

crimination between *ego* and *id* seems not so much discovery as foregone conclusion. The *id* (the term, incidentally, was borrowed from Nietzsche) embodies the instinctual passions, which the *ego*, like a man on horseback, must attempt to guide; the *ego*, champion of the reality of the external world, must constantly do battle with the *superego*, champion of the internal longings of the *id*. Dr. Jekyll spoke at least a decade in advance of Freud when he said "that man is not truly one, but truly two." From this multifarious awareness of the dichotomy in man's life, Carl Jung brings us back to the quincuncial dilemma of the present chapter with his observation that man as he matures must create around himself "a shell, which might be called a persona (mask)."[20]

Once such a deep rift has been struck between the internal and the external worlds of man's existence, the motif and image of mask can spring to vigorous life in the artistic imagination. Its simplest form is that which Jung's phrase suggests, the mask as protective shell, in Prufrock's words, the necessity "to prepare a face to meet the faces that you meet." Simply to strike a pose may be enough. "The first duty in life," proclaimed Oscar Wilde, "is to assume a pose; what the second is no one has yet

[20] Quotes from "Henry Jekyll's Full Statement of the Case," in "The Strange Case of Dr. Jekyll and Mr. Hyde"; and Jung, "The Relations Between the Ego and the Unconscious," in *Two Essays*, p. 160. To Jekyll's conclusion Freud would add, "The division of mental life into what is conscious and what is unconscious is the fundamental premise on which psycho-analysis is based." Sigmund Freud, *The Ego and the Id* (London: Hogarth, 1927), Chap. 1. Cf. William James, "What Psychical Research Has Accomplished," in *The Will To Believe* (New York: Longmans, Green, 1903): ". . . We all have potentially a 'subliminal' self, which may make at any time irruption into our ordinary lives."

found out."[21] Here we are in the presence of the dandyism of Wilde and Whistler and Walter Sickert. It is not simply the dandyism of a Disraeli or a Beau Brummel; it is dandyism with a purpose, a resolve (of which Matthew Arnold's manner of the 1830s and 1840s is the clearest forerunner) to shield and protect the inner self. It relates to other affected personalities of the age, such as Aubrey Beardsley's and Max Beerbohm's; William Gaunt is probably right in adding Walter Pater's mustache to the list.[22] The motif runs on to that passion for artificiality which stamps the age, most notably perhaps in the work of Arthur Symons, and in Max Beerbohm's defense of cosmetics, whereby "surface will finally be severed from soul."[23] Dorian Gray hides the horror and aging of his life beneath a mask of youth; Havelock Ellis scrutinizes his youthful

[21] Quotations from T. S. Eliot, "The Love Song of J. Alfred Prufrock" (1917) (cf. the motif earlier in Browning's two "soul-sides, one to face the world with," and one to show the beloved; Professor J. Hillis Miller, [*The Disappearance of God* (Cambridge: Harvard University Press, 1963), p. 101] observes that "each one of Browning's dramatic monologues is the playing of a role, the wearing of a mask."); and Wilde, from Ellmann, *Yeats: Man and Masks*, p. 71.

[22] *Aesthetic Adventure*, p. 52.

[23] "A Defence of Cosmetics," *Yellow Book*, I (April 1894). Cf. Baudelaire, "In Praise of Cosmetics," in *My Heart Laid Bare and Other Prose Writings* (London: George Weidenfield and Nicholson, 1950); William Butler Yeats, "Estrangement" (1909), Sect. 2, in *The Autobiography of William Butler Yeats* (New York: Doubleday, 1958); Wilde's letter to Philip Houghton, February 1894, in *The Letters of Oscar Wilde*, ed. Rupert Hart-Davis (London: Hart-Davis, 1962), p. 353; and Machen, *Hieroglyphics*, p. 180. Eugene O'Neill's *The Great God Brown* (1926) makes elaborate use of masks in this role of self-protection. George Orwell, in "The Art of Donald McGill" (1914), comments on "the ancient dualism of body and soul in fiction form."

visage in the mirror in an attempt to forestall the wrinkles of age or hardening of mind. Yeats labored for a style and a personality, a mask wherewith to "escape from the hot-faced bargainers and the money-changers" of a vulgar age, to shield a wounded spirit.[24]

There is an interesting connection here between the mask and the concurrent movement of symbolism. Based as it is upon analogy, not upon the one-to-one correspondence, the symbol's total meaning can never be "explained"; there will always be a discrepancy between the author's intention and the meaning attached to the symbol by his reader. But there is a point—at least sometimes—at which the symbol goes farther than this and serves not only to express the artist's "meaning," but also to disguise it. It may seem paradoxical of the artist, whom we might have expected to speak to us with effective clarity, thus willfully to withhold his meaning, yet the evidence of willful disguise is clear enough. Carlyle detects the point: "In a Symbol there is concealment and yet revelation." Edmund Wilson describes symbols as "a sort of disguise" for the artist's ideas.[25]

But we have still no answer to the question why. Why should the artist, whom many in this age had exalted to the role of priest, revert from revelation to deliberate concealment? Our discussion of masks gives some clue to the solution. "The symbol," writes a modern psychologist, "originates in the split of existence, the confrontation and

[24] References to Havelock Ellis, *My Life* (London: Heinemann, 1940), Chap. 3; and Yeats, "Estrangement" (1909), Sect. 2, in *Autobiography*.

[25] Quotations from Carlyle, *Sartor Resartus*, Bk. III, Chap. 3; and Wilson, *Axel's Castle* (New York: Scribner's, 1936), p. 20.

communication of an inner with an outer reality";[26] that is to say, the use and origin of the symbol lay partially in the very dichotomy that inspired the mask motif in this period. The symbol is an artistic device to suggest the inexpressible; it may also be—and often is—a device to protect the inner sensibility, to put off the intruder, to limit the world of one's inner life to those who are sensitive enough and closely enough akin to understand. From others, let us hide; let us speak a tongue they cannot know; let us, as in much of Yeats's later work, use the symbol as a mask.

Beyond this the mask, more than serving as a mere shield to protect one's sensitive inner life, takes on greater complexity. At a time when the phenomenal world increasingly seemed either unacceptable or incomprehensible, the need grew stronger to *project* the mode of being in which one would live. "A mask," said Yeats, "will enable me to substitute for the face of some commonplace player . . . the fine invention of a sculptor." One must proceed "as if" such things can be and can succeed, and so explore the limits to which one's personality may attain. For this projection of the personality which one wished to achieve, the technique and image of the mask fell pat to the artist's hand. It could be made to express his longing to live this short life more abundantly and diversely. In Wilde's view, disguises served this purpose for the murderer Thomas Griffiths Wainwright; they "intensified his personality."[27] The insincerity of the poses in

[26] Erich Kahler, "The Nature of the Symbol," in *Symbolism in Religion and Literature*, ed. Rollo May (New York: George Braziller, 1960), p. 53.
[27] Quotations from Yeats, "Certain Noble Plays of Japan" (1916),

Dorian Gray is a good thing; they form "a method by which we can multiply our personalities."[28] Indeed, A. H. Nethercot has made a good case for Wilde's having constructed *Dorian Gray* largely to show the interplay of projections of various aspects of Wilde's own personality. Arthur Symons thought of Wilde as continually making himself many souls.[29]

More significantly, the mask could provide the elevating means most apt to the current notion that man must draw himself onward and upward, and extend the reach of the Life Force to the fullest, lest he be displaced by some other, farther-reaching form of life. The mask in this role is most lucidly shown in Beerbohm's story of "The Happy Hypocrite," which appeared in the *Yellow Book* for October 1896. Here Lord George Hell, a hellion by both name and definition, assumes the mask of a saint in order to win the hand of a pure and noble maiden. He succeeds in his role and continues to play it. At his death he is unmasked and "lo! his face was even as his mask had been. Line for line, feature for feature, it was the same. 'Twas a saint's face." Yeats, also intrigued by the notion of mask, has his Player Queen make the same point: "To

in *Essays and Introductions* (New York: Macmillan, 1961), p. 226; and Wilde, "Pen, Pencil and Poison," in *Intentions* (1891), fourth paragraph.

[28] *Dorian Gray*, Chap. 11. For evidence that this view remains alive in contemporary literature, see Jessamyn West, "The Slave Cast Out," in *The Living Novel*, ed. Granville Hicks (New York: Macmillan, 1957), p. 202: "Writing is a way of playing parts, of trying on masks, of assuming roles, not for fun but out of desperate need. . . ."

[29] See Nethercot, "Oscar Wilde on His Subdividing Himself," *PMLA*, LX (June 1945), 616-617; and Symons, *A Study of Oscar Wilde* (London: C. J. Sawyer, 1930), p. 50.

be great we must seem so. Seeming that goes on for a life-time is no different from reality." As Virginia Moore puts it, "Project, fill out the projection—and lo! one stood taller."[30] Jung maintains that the boot-strap method will not work because one cannot make oneself what one is not, and Stanley Makower's Sarah Kaftal agrees.[31] But the matter is still arguable whether in a dischoate world the imaginative projection of one's highest self-conception, and the attempt to fulfill that conception, may not effectively exalt one's life to significance. Arthur Symons will answer yes: "The man who forces himself to appear calm under excitement teaches his nerves to follow instinctively the way he has shown them. In time he will not merely seem calm but will be calm. . . ." Professor Charlesworth disagrees and asserts that it was Symons' own inability to "find a 'mask' which would adequately define his intense self-consciousness" that led him to madness. My own inclination is to settle with George Santayana's conclusion: "Mask and buskin are often requisite in order to transport what is great in human experience out of its embosoming littleness. They are inseparable from finality, from perception of the ultimate."[32]

Finally, there is still another important role the mask played in the imagination and artistry of these years. It

[30] References are from Ellmann, *Yeats: Man and Masks*, p. 173; and Moore, *The Unicorn*, p. 213.

[31] See Jung, "The Persona as a Segment of the Collective Psyche," in "The Relations between the Ego and the Unconscious," in Jung, *Two Essays*, pp. 166-167; and Makower, *The Mirror of Music* (London, 1895), p. 68.

[32] Quotations from Symons, "Prosper Mérimée" (1901), Sect. II, in *Studies in Prose and Verse* (London, 1904); Charlesworth, *Dark Passages*, p. 98; and Santayana, "Preface" (1922) to *Poems* (New York: Scribner's, 1923), p. xi.

served to depersonalize the work of art and to remove the artist from his work. The motive seems contrary to the simultaneous move toward self-development and self-expression, and it is—but it was precipitated by the same cultural crisis. The impulse of the self-expressionist was to delight in the torrent of the unconscious, the will to power, the Life Force—whatever was taken to be the impulsive force behind all living things and all evolution's blind creations of the future. For the artist the impulse was—and is—to create and project from out of the flux something which, like a precious gem, is detached, beautiful, timeless, and something which succeeding generations could not destroy. In such an act of creation the artist must be remote, away—like Stephen Dedalus's "God of the creation, . . . refined out of existence, indifferent, paring his fingernails." In this vein Oscar Wilde would say, "Man is least himself when he talks in his own person. Give him a mask, and he will tell you the truth." Yeats called on his players to don masks "to eliminate the personality of the player from the play."[33] An interesting controversy arose in this time over the true nature of dramatic acting. Wilde, taking the mask as protection again, comments, "Perhaps one never seems so much at one's ease as when one has to play a part." But his own persona, Lord Henry Wotton, is closer to Wilde's true meaning when he says, "I love acting. It is so much more real than life."[34]

[33] Quotations from James Joyce, *The Portrait of the Artist as a Young Man*, Chap. 5; Wilde "The Critic as Artist," Pt. II, in *Intentions* (1891); and (regarding Yeats) St. John G. Ervine, *Some Impressions of My Elders* (London: Allen and Unwin, 1923), p. 265.

[34] The Wilde quotations are from *Dorian Gray*, Chaps. 15 and 6.

Or is this simply Lord Henry up to his old tricks by inverting the truth to attract attention? Is there an aesthetic validity to what he says? William Archer, for one, would have granted validity to Lord Henry's case. Archer's *Masks or Faces?* (1888) makes a careful, if indecisive, study of the question whether the best acting is a product of sincere emotional identification with the character one is recreating, or a product of sheer mimetic artifice. He observes that the first awareness that there might be two opinions on the matter arose in France in the mid-eighteenth century; previously it had been assumed that sincere emotional identification between actor and character was the consummation to be wished.[35] Archer examined memoirs of formerly great actors, interviewed others and used questionnaires to discover all he could of whether acting is genuine emotional identification or mere mimesis. His most interesting conclusions (Chapter 10 in his book) are that a great actor's mind operates on two levels as it performs, one part participating, the other alert to stagecraft. The book ends inconclusively, though perhaps mainly on the side of the *emotionalists*—those who insisted upon sincere identification with one's role as the best source of great acting. But one should keep the date of Archer's exploratory study in mind; the point is that *Masks or Faces?* dramatically raised the possibility that great art might be an affair of masks, and that in the mask, as in Eliot's "objective correlative," might be found

[35] Archer does cite, however (p. 26), Dr. Johnson's memorable pronouncement that ". . . If Garrick really believed himself to be that monster, Richard the Third, he deserved to be hanged every time he performed it." *Boswell's Life of Johnson*, ed. C. B. Tinker (2 vols., London: Oxford, 1934), p. 512.

a technique for communicating inner experience through objectification.

Thus the use of the mask thrived in the imagination of these decades (1) as protective shell to a wounded sensibility, (2) as a projective conception of the varieties and heights of being which man might achieve, and (3) as an aesthetic means for striking an aesthetic attitude, calm, fixed, serene, and outside the flux of time. In each of these roles the mask reveals its origin and the need of the imagination to cope with a world which left no place for human significance.

I have said that this study of the literary imagination in Britain between 1880 and 1914 makes no pretense at literary criticism. I do not seek to assess the aesthetic value of works or authors. Yet I submit that this study of the mask does demonstrate an imaginative and artistic affinity between two major Irish literary figures of the time— Oscar Wilde and William Butler Yeats. Both are "mask-haunted" writers. Wilde offered the classic response to Olive Schreiner's remark that she lived in the East End because there people wore no masks. ". . . I," rejoined Oscar, "live in the West End because they do."[36] Both Wilde and Yeats use the mask in the three fashions described above. Yeats, to be sure, was born eleven years later than Wilde, and his early years followed a different and more purposeful course of development; such factors may account in part for the striking difference in the qualities which the mask assumes in the two men's work.

The assets of the mask are apparent in Wilde. Dorian Gray and his portrait have all the surface attributes of a

---

[36] Ernest Rhys, *Everyman Remembers* (London: Dent, 1931), p. 103. A variation of the anecdote is told in Yeats, "Four Years," Bk. I, Sect. 17, in *Trembling of the Veil.*

Dostoevskian double. Wilde knew well, perhaps too well, the value of pose as an escape and a protection; he was aware that the use of the mask, as we have seen, could be a means of speaking the truth that would be far more effective for his time than the use of direct or lyric expression. But Wilde was capable of using the mask in downright cynicism, as in his play, *An Ideal Husband*, in which the dramatic value of Sir Robert Chiltern's posture of utter integrity is marred by the antithetical undercurrent of Wilde's socialism.[37] Worst of all, as André Gide observed, Wilde recurrently managed the mask "in such a way that the informed reader could raise [it] and glimpse, under it, the true visage." Wilde himself, in his *"De Profundis"* letter, makes the same point, that one must occasionally remove the mask, if only to breathe: "Else, indeed, you would be stifled."[38] It is just here, I believe, that the problem arises which many readers have felt with *"De Profundis"* and other works of Oscar Wilde—the aesthetic posture vacillates. Have we glimpsed beneath the mask in *"De Profundis"* and seen the "real" Oscar in deep remorse of conscience? Or do such glimpses reveal only a new mask, one of suffering and self-effacement? Even Wilde himself, I suspect, did not know. His "Ballad of Reading

[37] Sir Robert's role should be compared with Wilde's *"De Profundis"* letter to Lord Alfred Douglas, January-March 1897 (*Letters of Oscar Wilde*, pp. 487-488): "A man whose desire is to be something separate from himself, to be a Member of Parliament, or a successful grocer . . . invariably succeeds in what he wants to be. That is his punishment. Those who want a mask have to wear it."

[38] Quotations from *The Journals of André Gide*, trans. Justin O'Brien (4 vols., New York: Knopf, 1947-51), II, 409; and *"De Profundis"* letter to Lord Alfred Douglas, January-March 1897, in *Letters of Oscar Wilde*, p. 499.

Gaol," the most consistent in tone of his major poems, is flawed by this vacillation between two modes, as Yeats observes in the introduction to his *Oxford Book of Modern Verse* (1937).[39] Such vacillation pursues Wilde to the end of his days. The mask is ever with him, first concealing, then revealing, as is aptly demonstrated in his use of Sebastian Melmoth, a pseudonym wherein he combined the roles of martyred saint and fate-struck wanderer, pledged to the devil. One is tempted to conclude flatly that truly coherent artistic creation cannot be achieved amid such wavering uncertainty of role, however resourceful and inventive.

In Yeats the case is altered. None partook more deeply than he in the dichotomy of sensibility in his age, but he did not merely suffer it in anguish. In its very divisiveness he found a challenge to his art. In his young manhood he pondered long upon the faiths and doctrines which were fraught with duality—Hermetism, Blake's mystic creed, and the Druidism of Ireland.[40] He became acutely conscious of an antithesis in the human spirit, that each man had his double, an anti-self, which he must confront and come to terms with if he would be whole. Thus Christ came as "the antithetical self of the classic world."[41] In these ways Yeats drew strength from the division within himself, between poet and statesman, Michael Robartes

[39] It has not been previously noted, I think, that several motifs of the "Ballad," Sect. 3, have been imported from "The Harlot's House" (1883), another circumstance which argues against our reading the "Ballad" as the work of a wholly converted imagination.

[40] An excellent account of these youthful considerations is given in Moore, *The Unicorn*, Chaps. 3-7.

[41] "Anima Hominis," p. ix, in *Per Amica Silentia Lunae*.

and Owen Aherne; poet, dreamer, occultist *vs.* man of action. To this dichotomy Yeats later added a note with an overtone of existentialism: "I think of life as a struggle with the Daemon who would ever set us to the hardest work among those not impossible." (Cf. the cry of Hemingway's old man of the sea: "It is good that we do not have to try to kill the sun or the moon or the stars.") And with all this Yeats shared with Wilde and others of his time the insistence that art is something apart from the natural and the phenomenal world: "Art is art because it is not nature."[42]

To an artist steeped in this kind of antithesis, the mask could become, and did become, a masterful image. It could play not one role alone but many, and they might have, and did have, conflicting significances. (One cannot fence in the meaning of a symbol.) Thus one can understand how Yeats could claim that Napoleon triumphed because "he had some Roman emperor's image in his head and some condottiere's blood in his heart."[43] One can understand the source of Yeats's fascination with the Japanese Nō plays to which Ezra Pound introduced him; with their impassive masks and stylized movement, they were removed entirely from nature.[44] One can discover now the basis for Yeats's conviction that love itself creates and is the creation of the mask:

[42] Quotations from Yeats, *ibid.*, p. viiii (cf. Yeats, "Four Years," Bk. I, Sect. 24, in *Trembling of the Veil*); and Hemingway, *The Old Man and the Sea* (New York: Scribner's, 1952), p. 83; and Yeats, "The Tragic Generation," Bk. IV, Sect. 1, in *Trembling of the Veil*.

[43] "Four Years," Bk. I, Sect. 14, in *Trembling of the Veil*.

[44] See Frank Kermode, *Romantic Image* (New York: Chilmark, 1961), pp. 79-80. Cf. Baudelaire's longing for actors masked and raised on buskins; *My Heart Laid Bare*, p. 181.

"It was the mask engaged your mind,
And after set your heart to beat,
Not what's behind."

"What matter, so there is but fire
In you, in me?"[45]

(Can one resist the juxtaposition of Lord Henry Wotton's deflating comment: "When one is in love, one always begins by deceiving one's self, and one always ends by deceiving others.") In Yeats' careful art there is strong evidence to support his major pronouncements on the mask in *Dramatis Personae*: "I think that all happiness depends on the energy to assume the mask of some other self; that all joyous or creative life is a re-birth as something not oneself, something which has no memory and is created in a moment and perpetually renewed. . . .

"There is a relation between discipline and the theatrical sense. If we cannot imagine ourselves as different from what we are and assume that second self, we cannot impose a discipline upon ourselves, though we may accept one from others. Active virtue as distinguished from the passive acceptance of a current code is therefore theatrical, consciously dramatic, the wearing of a mask. It is the condition of arduous full life."[46]

Given the example of Yeats, who took this motif in the artistic life of his time and explored the depth and the range of its possibilities, the use of the mask, was touched by genius. The mask can protect the sensitivity

[45] Yeats's poem, "The Mask" (1910).
[46] Quotations from Wilde, *Dorian Gray*, Chap. 4; and Yeats, "The Death of Synge" (1909), and "Estrangement" (1909), Sect. 6, p. 340, and Sect. 22, p. 317, respectively, in *Autobiography*.

that is wounded and driven into isolation. It can reunite subject with object; for if the mask is aloof and impassive, it yet must have been born of the inner life of the one who created it. As Freud said of the ego and its "reality-principle," for all its objectivity it "constantly carries into action the wishes of the *id* as if they were its own."[47] And the mask, in a vacuous world, can project an ideal capable of drawing the artist's spirit into purposeful action. Not the artistic spirit only. If one is dismayed in our own time over a world that seemingly operates according to the bare dictates of economics and power, that looks upon "escalation" with helpless passivity, and that lets occasion inform all policy, then one may well heed Yeats's words on the mask. They are the more persuasive since in his own active life they did give strength to his native land and did assist in reshaping its destiny: "Nations, races, and individual men are unified by an image, or bundle of related images, symbolical or evocative of the state of mind, which is of all states of mind not impossible, the most difficult to that man, race, or nation; because only the greatest obstacle that can be contemplated without despair rouses the will to full intensity."[48]

[47] *The Ego and the Id*, Chap. 2.
[48] "Four Years," Bk. I, Sect. 24, in *Trembling of the Veil*.

CHAPTER 7

Ecstasy

It will seem rash to take as a second symptomatic motif of these transformative years the theme of ecstasy. Ecstasy has been woven into human experience for as long as time remembers; certainly it was there with the Greeks, who (naturally) first had a word for it. To be out of place, to be removed from one's habitual being, to be "beside oneself." Marghanita Laski's definition is adequate to the purpose of the present study: ecstasy comprises ". . . a range of experiences characterized by being joyful, transitory, unexpected, rare, valued, and extraordinary to the point of often seeming as if derived from a praeternatural source."[1] Miss Laski's study of ecstasy is illuminating and highly suggestive, and her illustrations of the experience confirm the fact that it is known to many cultures and to many centuries.

In the record of English emotional experience, it is the religious ecstasy that has the longest tradition. The illuminations of the saint and the intense rapture of the mystic are amply recorded in the Middle Ages and the Renaissance. From the seventeenth century, Traherne's meditations come to mind, and Donne's ecstasies, with their passionate ambivalence, semi-sensual, semi-mystical. From the eighteenth century, there is Smart's "Song to David." And William James's *The Varieties of Religious Experience* (1902) gives evidence that in the nineteenth

[1] Marghanita Laski, *Ecstasy: A Study in Some Secular and Religious Experiences* (London: Cresset Press, 1961), p. 5.

century ecstasy could still be experienced as a glorious moment of confirmation in man's spiritual life. "I have stood upon the Mount of Vision . . . ," one clergyman wrote to James, "and felt the Eternal round about me," and "my highest faith in God and truest idea of him were then born in me."[2] We shall find, too, that the spiritual ecstasy persists in imaginative literature at the turn of the century.

Nevertheless, the intensity and the character of the ecstatic experience in literature do alter markedly and symptomatically in the nineteenth century, and particularly at its close. One might fairly contend to begin with that the ecstasy of the secular literary imagination is virtually born with the Romantic movement. Miss Laski's random sampling of religious and literary texts gives some clue to this. Of her twenty-four religious texts, only five date later than 1800; of her thirty literary texts, only one (Ovid!) is pre-1800. It takes but a moment's reflection to confirm that in Romantic writing the *instant* of ecstatic revelation became a focus of longing and aspiration.

> To see a world in a grain of sand,
> And a heaven in a wild flower;
> Hold infinity in the palm of your hand,
> And eternity in an hour.[3]

Since orthodox faiths seemed to provide at best a waning assurance of any real contact with what is permanent, unified, or harmonious beyond the phenomenal world, it is as though the poet sought more insistently to find such experience through the imagination. Keats may be the most

[2] *The Varieties of Religious Experience: A Study in Human Nature* (1902) (New York: Modern Library, n.d.), p. 66.
[3] William Blake, "Auguries of Innocence" (ca. 1803).

poignant example, in his longing to fly away with the nightingale, or to share the wild ecstasy of the Bacchic throng on the Grecian urn. But with Keats a magnificent sense of reality draws the poet back from the vision and holds him close to earth, to warmth and transiency; the exaltation fades, leaving him forlorn and desolate. For Shelley the ecstatic flight has lighter chains; he wrote to John Gisborne in 1821, "As to real flesh & blood, you know that I do not deal in those articles,—you might as well go to a ginshop for a leg of mutton, as expect anything human or earthly from me."[4] The fifth stanza of Shelley's "Hymn to Intellectual Beauty" (1816) is his most explicit record of Romantic ecstasy:

> Sudden, thy shadow fell on me;
> I shrieked, and clasped my hands in ecstasy!

Shelley vowed to live by that experience, to dedicate his powers "to thee and thine," and he kept his vow. He may have lamented in later years that the spirit of delight came less often to him, but he never lost faith in that eternal intellectual beauty which his ecstasies had revealed.

The Romantic poet most deeply imbued with and shaped by the experience of ecstasy is of course William Wordsworth. In Wordsworth the heart of the man and the mind of the poet find their motive in moments of ecstasy—in rowing or skating on the Cumberland lakes, rolling into London on the top of the Cambridge coach, climbing Snowdon some summer night, or musing on the hillside above Tintern Abbey. Such moments—these "spots of time"—came from distinctive, recurring sources

[4] Letter of October 22, 1821, in Frederick L. Jones, ed., *The Letters of Percy Bysshe Shelley* (2 vols., Oxford: Clarendon Press, 1964), II, 363.

in Wordsworth's experience, moments of rapid motion, climbing upward, hearing sounds across water, and solitude. These are moments when

> ... with an eye made quiet by the power
> Of harmony, and the deep power of joy,
> We see into the life of things.

In later years of stress and disillusionment, it was the subjective recollection of such moments—memories of ecstasy—which sustained the fabric of Wordsworth's philosophy:

> O joy! that in our embers
> Is something that doth live,
> That Nature yet remembers
> What was so fugitive!

In Wordsworth most of all it is apparent that the Romantics sought, through ecstatic moments of vision, a new religion not shackled by dogmatic Christianity, although their ecstasies recurrently showed what Professor Rosenberg has called "an unconscious pilfering from modes of Christian experience."[5] In ecstasy the Romantics found their best assurance of the eternal, the true, and the beautiful—ideals they sought to live by and, in their poetry, to reveal.

[5] Quotations from Wordsworth, "Tintern Abbey" (1798); his "Ode: Intimations of Immortality," Sect. ix (1804); and John D. Rosenberg, *The Darkening Glass: A Portrait of Ruskin's Genius* (New York: Columbia University Press, 1961), p. 20. Ernest de Selincourt, in the "Introduction" to his edition of *The Prelude* (London: Oxford, 1925), p. lvii, asserts that in the early 1800s, "Wordsworth's faith was in no way tinged with dogmatic Christianity." Jonathan Bishop, "Wordsworth and the 'Spots of Time,'" *ELH*, XXVI (March 1959), 45-65, provides an excellent study of Wordsworthian ecstasies.

One could go further in exploring the Romantic ecstasy to consider, as Professor Abrams has done, the uses of opium to induce freedom from the limitations of time and space.[6] To De Quincey, opium brought moments in which there were "motions of the intellect as unwearied as the heavens, yet for all anxieties a halcyon calm; a tranquility that seemed no product of inertia, but as if resulting from mighty and equal antagonisms; infinite activities, infinite repose." Or one could look to the Brontës, Emily and Charlotte, and their ecstasies of the moors, such as Jane Eyre's flight from Thornfield, across the heath at night: "Night was come, and her planets were risen. . . . Certainly we feel [God's] presence most when His works are on the grandest scale spread before us; and it is in the unclouded night sky, where His worlds wheel their silent course, that we read clearest His infinitude, His omnipotence, His omnipresence. . . . Sure was I of His efficiency to save what He had made; convinced I grew that neither earth should perish, nor one of the souls it treasured." It is the survival of the Wordsworthian ecstasy and the continuing of his faith

> . . . that Nature never did betray
> The heart that loved her.[7]

But the problem is to demonstrate that the ecstasies of

[6] Meyer Howard Abrams, *The Milk of Paradise: The Effect of Opium Visions on the Works of De Quincey, Crabbe, Francis Thompson, and Coleridge* (Cambridge, Mass.: Harvard University Press, 1934).

[7] Quotations from Thomas de Quincey, "The Pleasures of Opium" (penultimate paragraph), in *Confessions of an English Opium-Eater* (1822); Charlotte Brontë, *Jane Eyre*, Chap. 28; and Wordsworth, "Tintern Abbey."

the literary imagination in the late nineteenth and early twentieth centuries do change in intensity and character, and that the change is explicable in terms of the cultural crisis which has been described. It is my contention that the ecstasies in literature at the turn of the century show three marked alterations from those of the earlier tradition. The longing for ecstatic experience became vastly more urgent, and hence the records of ecstasy become far more pervasive in literature and are apt to spring from, be "triggered" by, more diverse motives and conditions. Second, the ecstasy came to be considered less as a *means* —of glimpsing God, or Intellectual Beauty, or "that immortal sea/Which brought us hither"[8]—and more as an *end* in itself, frequently as an avowed escape. Third, the ecstasies of this time were prized more for the subjective rewards they brought than for their confirmation of some higher harmony or for their promise of some brighter sphere which may exist behind and beyond the phenomenal world known to man. I hope to show that these three things are true and, in the light of earlier pages, that they are significantly true.

Perhaps the ecstasies of literature in this period may be separated into kinds. (I feel gently twitted by Hans Vaihinger's comment nearly contemporary with my subject: "Understanding is the well-known feeling of pleasure due to the empirical transformation of sensations into categories."[9]) But our focus will be clearer if the kinds of ecstasies are distinguished, and the distinction should reinforce one

[8] Wordsworth, "Ode: Intimations of Immortality," Sect. IX (1804).

[9] *The Philosophy of "As If,"* trans. C. K. Ogden (London: Routledge and Kegan Paul, 1952), p. 171. This portion of Vaihinger's work was in manuscript as early as 1877.

of my contentions, that there is striking diversity in the modes of ecstasy in this literature.

First of all, the spiritual ecstasy continues in the literary imagination of the turn of the century; indeed I suspect it is intensified by that urge for fervent faith which impelled the Oxford Movement, neo-Catholicism, and the heightening of ritual in the Anglican church service in the nineteenth century. Evidence of religious ecstasy is most vividly seen in Gerard Manley Hopkins. Many of his greatest short poems—"The Windhover," "Pied Beauty," "Hurrahing in Harvest"—are epiphanies of spiritual inspiration.

> Soul, self; come, poor Jackself, I do advise
> You, jaded, let be; call off thoughts awhile
> Elsewhere; leave comfort root-room; let joy size
> At God knows when to God know what; whose smile
> 's not wrung, see you; unforeseen times rather—as skies
> Betweenpie mountains—lights a lovely mile.[10]

Hopkins feels the dryness of the bare, trodden world; his spirit yearns and quickens to "stress, instress" the mystery that yet lurks there. He catches the inscape of act or scene; its beauty stirs him, and the moment explodes into revelation—"the achieve of, the mastery of the thing!" Francis Thompson's poetry, too, gives recurrent evidence of spiritual epiphany and the confirmation through ecstasy of a divine world invisible beyond our own.

> Not where the wheeling systems darken,
> And our benumbed conceiving soars!—
> The drift of pinions, would we hearken,
> Beats at our own clay-shuttered doors.

[10] Sonnet, "My own heart let me more have pity on" (1885).

The angels keep their ancient places;—
Turn but a stone, and start a wing!
'Tis ye, 'tis your estranged faces,
That miss the many-splendoured thing.

But (when so sad thou canst not sadder)
Cry;—and upon thy so sore loss
Shall shine the traffic of Jacob's ladder
Pitched betwixt Heaven and Charing Cross.[11]

It remained for Arthur Machen to give a critical rationale to the spiritual ecstasy in the new age. He takes *ecstasy* as the mark and touchstone of all great literature, since ecstasy alone strikes through to the unconscious and subconscious, that is to say, to "the enduring facts of human nature and the universe." And to Machen, the Catholic Church is the earthly spokesman for these facts: "Yes, it is really so . . ."; ". . . Literature is the expression, through the aesthetic medium of words, of the dogmas of the Catholic Church, and that which is in any way out of harmony with those dogmas is not literature." "To make literature it is necessary to be, at all events subconsciously, Catholic."[12]

A second, far more pervasive mode of ecstasy at the turn of the century originated from a vision of earth. It was a frequent response of the imagination in the post-Darwinian world to celebrate man's new kinship with all life and with the earth from which he came. I have indi-

[11] Thompson, "The Kingdom of God."

[12] *Hieroglyphics* (London: Unicorn, 1960), pp. 179, 176-177, 179.
It may expand the range of spiritual ecstasy in literature again to be reminded that ". . . all mystics of all religions ultimately attain to a kind of ecstasy." Schopenhauer, *The World as Will and Idea*, III, 430 n.

cated this motif before. In the ecstasies of earth there are similarities to and reminders of Wordsworth, but the higher harmony which is implied and reached for has become manifestly more amorphous and remote—a limitless immensity, the "mystic bellbird" of Hudson's *Green Mansions,* the "enchanted woods" of Meredith's Westermain. Perhaps in the greater vagueness of its idealistic context, the ecstasy of nature does become more accessible to the literary imagination. Certainly in this generation it is prevalent in many authors and in many works.

For Havelock Ellis it was this kind of ecstasy which restored his vitality and gave direction to his whole life's work. He tells in his autobiography of the "conversion" which came upon him by Sparkes Creek, deep in the Australian bush. He had been reading James Hinton's *Life in Nature,* and suddenly the clash in his inner life between scientific conceptions and a "divine vision of life and beauty" was resolved. "An immense inner transformation had been effected, as it seemed, in a moment."[13] A picture of the bend of Sparkes Creek, where this transformation took place, remained at Ellis's bedside throughout his life. A similar, though more prolonged, experience lay behind Edward Carpenter's finding of his faith in *Towards Democracy*: "It seemed all ready there. I never hesitated for a moment. . . . The one illuminating mood remained and everything fell into place under it. . . . What sweet times were those! all the summer to the hum of the bees in the leafage, the robins and chaffinches hopping around, an occasional large bird flying by, the men

[13] *My Life* (London: William Heinemann, 1940), pp. 130-131; Chap. 4 of this work gives the full account of Ellis's "conversion."

away at work in the fields. . . . There was a sense of in-
evitableness in it all, and of being borne along. . . ."[14]

As the ecstasy of kinship with earth came into the literature of this time, it appeared in various modes. In
D. H. Lawrence it is sexual love that most dramatically
reveals the underlying harmony: "As a rule, when he
started love-making, the emotion was strong enough to
carry with it everything—reason, soul, blood—in a great
sweep. . . . Gradually the little criticisms, the little sensations, were lost, thought also went, everything borne along
in one flood. . . . It was as if he, and the stars, and the
dark herbage, and Clara were licked up in an immense
tongue of flame, which tore onwards and upwards. Everything rushed along in living beside him; everything was
still, perfect in itself, along with him. This wonderful
stillness in each thing in itself, while it was being
borne along in a very ecstasy of living, seemed the highest
point of bliss.

". . . It was all so much bigger than themselves that he
was hushed. They had met, and included in their meeting
the thrust of the manifold grass stems, the cry of the pee-
wit, the wheel of the stars."[15] For others, the ecstasy of

[14] *My Days and Dreams* (London: Allen and Unwin, 1921),
Chap. 5, pp. 106-107.
[15] *Sons and Lovers* (1913) (New York: Viking, 1960), Chap. 13,
pp. 363-364. Cf. Lawrence's statement in "Edgar Allan Poe,"
Chap. 6 of *Studies in Classic American Literature* (1923) (New
York: Doubleday, 1953), p. 86: ". . . We all want this spiritual
gratification, this flow, this apparent heightening of life, this
knowledge, this valley of many-coloured grass, even grass and
light prismatically decomposed, giving ecstasy. We want all this
without resistance. We want it continually. And this is the root
of all evil in us."

earth was a revelation of eternity, perhaps an analogue to the aesthete's search for permanence in the world of art— "that little city of gold where the flute-player never wearies, and the spring never fades. . . ." In this mode is "the sense of personal everlastingness" that John Davidson felt as he walked in the forest, and Richard Jefferies' discovery that the hills of his homeland were "alive with the dead" (not surprisingly, since Jefferies' land was the land of Stonehenge, Avebury, and Windmill Hill). The sense of everlastingness could in turn be transmuted to ecstasy, as Andrew Peak's musing, in Gissing's *Born in Exile*, on the geological strata laid bare in a roadside quarry: "Then a strange fit of brooding came over him. Escaping from the influences of personality, his imagination wrought back through eras of geologic time, held him in a vision of the infinitely remote, shrivelled into insignificance all but the one fact of inconceivable duration. Often he had lost himself in such reveries, never yet had he passed so wholly under the dominion of that awe which attends a sudden triumph of the pure intellect."[16]

But the major theme of ecstasy in nature is defined most clearly in Hudson and Jefferies; the "New Antaeanism" is manifest in all their work. Abel in *Green Mansions* hears the note of the bellbird and is swept to "a sense of an impersonal, all-compromising One who is in me and I in him, flesh of his flesh and soul of his soul. The sounds

[16] Quotations from Wilde, letter to R. H. Sherard, May 17, 1883, in *The Letters of Oscar Wilde*, ed. Rupert Hart-Davis (London: Hart-Davis, 1962), p. 147; Davidson, "Hadley Wood," *Glasgow Herald*, October 20, 1894, p. 7; Edward Thomas, *Richard Jefferies: His Life and Work* (London, 1909), p. 7; and Gissing, Pt. I, Chap. 3 (cf. Pt. VI, Chap. 3).

ceased, but I was still in that exalted mood, and, like a person in a trance, staring fixedly before me." This dream-state of union with the universal consciousness of nature was a part of Richard Jefferies' experience from early childhood on: "I looked at the hills, at the dewy grass, and then up through the elm branches to the sky. In a moment all that was behind me, the house, the people, the sounds, seemed to disappear, and to leave me alone. Involuntarily I drew a long breath, then I breathed slowly. My thought, or inner consciousness, went up through the illumined sky, and I was lost in a moment of exaltation. This only lasted a very short time, perhaps only part of a second, and while it lasted there was no formulated wish. I was absorbed; I drank the beauty of the morning; I was exalted." The passage recalls Marius' epiphany in the Sabine hills, that "peculiar and privileged hour" when all fell precisely into focus. And, of course, all such passages recall Whitman:

> Swiftly rose and spread around me the peace and
>   knowledge that pass all the argument of the earth,
> And I know that the hand of God is the promise of
>   my own,
> And I know that the spirit of God is the brother of
>   my own,
> And that all the men ever born are also my brothers,
>   and the women my sisters and lovers,
> And that a kelson of the creation is love. . . .[17]

[17] Quotations from William Henry Hudson, *Green Mansions* (1904), Chap. 10; Richard Jefferies, *Story of My Heart* (1883), Chap. 5 (cf. Chap. 12: "Sometimes a very ecstasy of exquisite enjoyment of the entire visible universe filled me. I was aware that in reality the feeling and the thought were in me, and not in the earth

There is no more fertile inspiration to ecstasy at the turn of the century than in the imagination gone to earth.

A third kind of ecstasy found its source in the creed of aestheticism itself. How else are we to account for the scriptural authority which was accorded to Pater's "Conclusion," in which he asks the reader to ". . . be present always at the focus where the greatest number of vital forces unite in their purest energy. . . . To burn always with this hard, gemlike flame, to maintain this ecstasy, is success in life."? Through art the aesthetes promised to enrapture everyone with a still and perfect world beyond our own. The ecstasy could be caught in parody, as with Sir William Gilbert's view of the aesthete enraptured—"How Botticellian! How Fra Angelican! . . . They are indeed jolly utter!"—or in Yeats's serious avowal that it is the aim of poetry, by its rhythm, to induce trance, and to become in itself "a kind of ecstasy." Most significantly, the aesthetic ecstasy appears in the Joycean epiphany; the very word "epiphany" reminds us of the tendency of secular ecstasies to pilfer religious experience, as Joyce describes: "First we recognise that the object is *one* integral thing, then we recognise that it is an organised composite structure, a *thing* in fact: finally, when the relation of the parts is exquisite, when the parts are adjusted to the special point, we recognise that it is *that* thing which it is. Its soul, its whatness, leaps up to us from the vestment of its appearance. The soul of the commonest object, the structure of which is so adjusted, seems to us

---

or sun; yet I was more conscious of it when in company with these."); Pater, *Marius the Epicurean*, Chap. 19; and Whitman, *Leaves of Grass* (1885), Sect. 5.

radiant. The object achieves its epiphany."[18] Such moments of epiphany, "lightnings of intuition," inspire and illumine Stephen Dedalus as he seeks his mission in life; an example is his encounter with the birdlike girl on the seashore: ". . . Heavenly God! cried Stephen's soul, in an outburst of profane joy.

"He turned away from her suddenly and set off across the strand. His cheeks were aflame; his body was aglow; his limbs were trembling. On and on and on he strode, far out over the sands, singing wildly to the sea, crying to greet the advent of the life that had cried to him.

". . . A wild angel had appeared to him, the angel of mortal youth and beauty, an envoy from the fair courts of life, to throw open before him in an instant of ecstasy the gates of all the ways of error and glory. On and on and on and on!" Joyce based his art on such moments of epiphany, as Virginia Woolf did also—those "little daily miracles, illuminations, matches struck unexpectedly in the dark."[19] In the crisis of intensified sensibility—what

[18] The three quotations are from Gilbert and Sullivan, *Patience*, Act II; Yeats's lecture of May 29, 1903, as recorded in Henry W. Nevinson, *Changes and Chances* (London: Nisbet, 1923), pp. 302-303 (cf. the concluding paragraph of Yeats's essay, "The Autumn of the Body" [1898], and "Discoveries" [1906], in *Essays and Introductions* [New York: Macmillan, 1961], p. 294 and T. J. Cobden-Sanderson, *The Arts and Crafts Movement* [London, 1905], pp. 35-36); and Joyce, *Stephen Hero*, p. 190 (cf. pp. 188, 199).

[19] The quotations are from Joyce, *The Portrait of the Artist As a Young Man*, Chap. 4; Woolf, *To the Lighthouse* (London: Harcourt, Brace and World, 1927), Pt. III, Sect. III. Harry Levin ("Reflections on the Final Volume of the Oxford History of English Literature," I, *Forum for Modern Language Studies* [January 1965], p. 9) names Yeats's "Adoration of the Magi" as a source for Joyce's conception of the epiphany.

Yeats calls the "moment of passionate experience"[20]—the mundane and habitual is for an instant linked with eternity, and transiency, despair, and vacuity seem momentarily left behind.

The language of these expressions of ecstasy, and the very definition with which we began, make it clear that this motif runs directly into the high value put on *the moment* in relatively recent literature. Examples are everywhere—in Woolf; in Forster, where "the moment . . . stands for some eternal principle. We accept it, at whatever costs, and we have accepted life. But if we reject it, the moment, so to speak, passes; the symbol is never offered again."[21] The impulse is apparent in T. S. Eliot's (and Joyce's) search for a quiet center in life's chaos:

> At the still point of the turning world. Neither
>   flesh nor fleshless;
> Neither from nor towards; at the still point, there
>   the dance is,
> But neither arrest nor movement.[22]

Finally, the ecstasies of the turn of the century often

[20] Yeats, "Hodos Chameliontos," Bk. III, Sect. 7, in *Trembling of the Veil*, in *The Autobiography of William Butler Yeats* (New York: Doubleday, 1958).

[21] E. M. Forster, *The Longest Journey* (New York: Vintage, 1922), Pt. I, p. 149. Cf. Forster's story, "The Eternal Moment," in which "the moment" had "more reality in it than in all the years of success and varied achievement which had followed, and which it had rendered possible."

[22] "Burnt Norton" (1935). Ethel F. Cornwell, in *The 'Still Point'* (New Brunswick: Rutgers University Press, 1962), has valuably compared and contrasted the themes of the "ecstatic moment," the "moment of reality," and "the still point of the turning world" as manifest in the work of T. S. Eliot, Coleridge, Yeats, Henry James, Woolf, and Lawrence.

mark the period's new awareness of subconscious and unconscious elements in human experience. For William
James the discovery of the subliminal consciousness was
"the most important step forward that [had] occurred in
psychology" in his time, and the discovery lent inspiration and justification to many modes of ecstatic experience. ". . . Ecstasy and anguish," wrote Havelock Ellis,
"are the life-blood of the world."[23] R. M. Bucke interpreted
his illuminating vision, when in a flash he beheld "that the
foundation principle of the world is what we call love and
that the happiness of every one is in the long run absolutely
certain," as a moment of that "cosmic consciousness"
which was gradually evolving in all mankind.[24] Once
that thesis is presented in Bucke's *Cosmic Consciousness*,
the book becomes a collection of such visionary ecstasies.
For Yeats the ecstasy of poet and poem was often associated with a state like a hypnotic trance and with his own
experiences with spiritism and the occult. Edward Carpenter found affinities between revelations in his own life
and the mysticism of the orient, that universal consciousness where "individual self and life thin away to a mere
film, and are only the shadows cast by the glory revealed
beyond." Even Freud, quizzed by a correspondent, was
forced to come to terms with those moments of "oceanic
feeling" which others—not he—had experienced. He sug-

[23] Quotations from *Varieties of Religious Experience*, p. 228;
and Havelock Ellis, *Impressions and Comments: Second Series,
1914-1920* (London: Constable, 1921), p. 183.

[24] *Cosmic Consciousness* (Philadelphia, 1901), p. 10. Edward
Carpenter (*From Adam's Peak to Elephanta* [London, 1892], p.
155) notes that to attain cosmic consciousness "one must have the
power of knowing one's self separate from the body, of passing
into a state of ecstasy in fact."

gested that such moments may be hangovers from "an early stage in ego-feeling," when "the ego includes everything."[25] It is immediately apparent what a vast chasm lay between the culture after and the culture before these decades, between the ecstasy as intriguing psychic phenomenon and the ecstasy which touched on the eternal, between Freud's "oceanic feeling" and Wordsworth's reach for eternity, through

> sight of that immortal sea
> Which brought us hither.

Perhaps there is no writer of this period whose work is more insistently marked by the hunger for ecstasy than Arthur Symons. His poems touch again and again on the themes of "the ecstasy of love's unrest," "the rapture of a tragic ecstasy," "the ecstasy of Death."[26] One example may serve, since it brings together the sensuous frenzy of these shifting years, their fascination with the dance, and this present theme of ecstasy:

> For the immortal moment of a passionate dance,
> Surely our two souls rushed together and were one,
> Once, in the beat of our winged feet in unison,
> When, in the brief and flaming ardour of your glance,
> The world withered away, vanishing into smoke;
> The world narrowed about us, and we heard the beat
> As of the rushing winds encompassing our feet;
> In the blind heart of the winds, eternal silence woke,

---

[25] The three quotations are from Carpenter, *ibid.*, p. 155; and Freud, *Civilization and Its Discontents* (London: Hogarth, 1955), pp. 20, 13.

[26] These three phrases are from Symons's poems "Stella Maris" (1893); "Mundi Victima" (1896), Stanza IV; and "Wine of Circe" (1895).

And, cast adrift on our unchainable ecstasy,
Once, and once only, heart to heart, and soul to soul,
For an immortal moment we endured the whole
Rapture of intolerable immortality.[27]

It is needless to dissect, or to categorize further. The ecstasies of the turn of the century have at least four distinguishable sources, in a religious vision, in a oneness with nature, in aesthetic creed or in a faith in the subconscious. The modes are comprehended in a larger unity, a cultural climate in which the experience of ecstasy was intensely, at times indiscriminately, longed for, as a subjective good, an end in itself, a justifying reward in a world in which rewards were few. Are they revelations of a higher reality, or simply moments of intensity in man's earthbound sensory experience? Often one cannot tell, and perhaps the significant point in this age of transition is that the question is unanswerable. The ecstasy of Will Brangwen, in Lawrence's *The Rainbow* (Chap. 7), gives a final unifying example: "He had pushed open the doors of the cathedral, and entered the twilight of both darknesses, the hush of the two-fold silence, where dawn was sunset, and the beginning and the end were one.

"Here the stone leapt up from the plain of earth, leapt up in a manifold, clustered desire each time, up, away from the horizontal earth, through twilight and dusk and the whole range of desire, through the swerving, the declination, ah, to the ecstasy, the touch, to the meeting and the consummation, the meeting, the clasp, the close embrace, the neutrality, the perfect, swooning consummation, the timeless ecstasy. There his soul remained, at the

[27] Symons, "The Dance" (1895).

apex of the arch, clinched in the timeless ecstasy, consummated."

It only remains to ask *why*, in the light of our larger view of the crisis of this period, such a rage for ecstasy should prevail in its literature. I suggest that the loss of the idealistic bearings of man's spiritual and imaginative life does precipitate and inflict on him the necessity to find elsewhere, or to fabricate, the consolations which that lost idealism had given. The drift toward just such a necessity may be seen in the Pre-Raphaelites of the 1850s, '60s, and '70s. Professor Charlesworth writes well of Dante Gabriel Rossetti's role in the transition: "His emotions cried out for the existence of a transcendent realm while his reason questioned its existence." Symons observed that in Rossetti "all energy is concentrated on the one ecstasy, and this exists for its own sake. . . ."[28] The collapse of all belief in the transcendent in the ensuing decades accounts largely, in my opinion, for the urgency and pervasiveness of this quest for ecstasy—in absinthe or hashish, in love or in sensuousness, in art or in reverie—in the imaginative life of this time.

Then, too, the contemporary disillusionment with the intellect, the "retreat from reason," put greater value on emotional experience. One might simply say that the certainties which earlier Victorians had sought through reason had now to be sought elsewhere, and by other means. William James explicitly recommended the cure: "The

[28] Quotations from Barbara Charlesworth, *Dark Passages: The Decadent Consciousness in Victorian Literature* (Madison: University of Wisconsin Press, 1965), p. 16; and Arthur Symons, "Dante Gabriel Rossetti," in *Figures of Several Centuries* (London: Constable, 1917). Miss Charlesworth's entire chapters on Rossetti and Swinburne are relevant in this connection.

peace of rationality may be sought through ecstasy when logic fails."[29] This must explain why the ecstasies of the turn of the century seem to be less a means for perceiving an external reality than ends in themselves.[30] Here is an interesting analogy to the point Professor Houghton convincingly makes in his section on "Aspiration without an Object" in the earlier Victorian period. He finds evidence of a motif in which "the eye is focused not on an ideal but on oneself in glorious pursuit of an ideal—some ideal or other." We should also recall Robert Browning's faith in the supreme moment in man's existence where he is tested, where his real stature is measured. The difference in late-century ecstasy is that it was more emotional, less purposefully energetic, and it lacked the insistent upward surge of aspiration; there was more escapism in it, and more willful, even blind, immersement in sensation. The rage for ecstasy is clearly linked to the frenetic quality of the literary imagination, especially in the 1890s. "The age demanded . . . the climacteric moments only when the passions of the personae were at white heat, . . . and life was lived intensely."[31] It may have been Pater's recommendation of a life of sustained ecstasy that made Yeats rather fearful of Pater's influence, and fearful that it may have spelt tragedy

[29] "The Sentiment of Rationality," in *The Will to Believe and Other Essays in Popular Philosophy* (London: Longmans, Green, 1903), p. 74.

[30] Note that such appeals of ecstasy readily took precedence over those of ethics. As Yeats wrote to Dorothy Wellesley: "People much occupied with morality always lose heroic ecstasy." Letter dated July 6, 1934, in *The Letters of W. B. Yeats*, ed. Allan Wade (New York: Macmillan, 1955), p. 836.

[31] Quotations from Walter E. Houghton, *Victorian Frame of Mind: 1830-1870* (New Haven: Yale University Press, 1957), p. 292; and Bernard Muddiman, *The Men of the Nineties* (London: Henry Danielson, 1920), pp. 60-61.

for the generation of his disciples: "It taught us to walk upon a rope, tightly stretched through serene air, and we were left to keep our feet upon a swaying rope in a storm."[32]

Finally, and perhaps most lastingly, the quest for ecstasy was induced by the new relativism, the growing conviction among scientists and all thinking men that the world is not fully intelligible to human reason. If man's grasp of objective reality is to be broken, subjective reality becomes correspondingly more important; it is in the subjective that man must live to find the "real" realities, the courage to be, and the strength to dream. The ecstasy now becomes not that of the mystic, not that of Thompson's vision of

> . . . the traffic of Jacob's ladder
> Pitched betwixt Heaven and Charing Cross;

rather it is the artist's perception of the radiance—a radiance which he himself may both discover and create—of an inner reality. The truth, as Kierkegaard believed, must be created anew within us every day. As a psychologist of our own time has said, "From the very start, existence is rather the 'ecstatic' relationship, a true 'being' with the things of the world, a constant revelation, and a continual opening of doors." But long before this an artist has said it: "The end of art is the ecstasy awakened by the presence before an ever-changing mind of what is permanent in the world, or by the arousing of that mind itself into the very delicate and fastidious mood habitual with it when it is seeking those permanent and recurring

[32] Yeats, "The Tragic Generation," Bk. IV, Sect. 5, in *Trembling of the Veil.*

things."[33] One is tempted to read the ecstasies in literature at the turn of the century as steps toward the realization and establishment of this truth.

The result of all this preoccupation with ecstatic experience was substantially to affect the conception of the role of art and the artist in the period from 1880 to 1914. There were prophets abroad to establish the point in theory. "To the existence of art," said Nietzsche, "to the existence of any aesthetic activity or perception whatsoever, a preliminary psychological condition is indispensable, namely, *ecstasy*." For Bergson art springs from "volcanic eruptions, ... sudden explosions whereby [the earth] suddenly resumes possession of its innermost nature." Yeats saw well enough that there might be in poetry "an almost disembodied ecstasy." And also Arthur Machen: "If ecstasy be present, then I say there is fine literature; if it be absent, then, in spite of all the cleverness, all the talents, all the workmanship and observation and dexterity you can show me, then, I think, we have a product ... which is not fine literature."[34] Thence to the artist, to Yeats and

[33] Quotations from Thompson, "The Kingdom of God"; Yeats, "Discoveries," in Yeats, *Essays and Introductions*, p. 287; and Medard Bass, *The Analysis of Dreams*, trans. Arnold J. Pomerans (New York: Philosophical Library, 1958), p. 164. For the reference to Bass, as for several larger insights into this period, I am indebted to Professor Morse Peckham.

[34] Quotations from Nietzsche, "Roving Expeditions of an Inopportune Philosopher," Sect. 8, in *Twilight of the Idols*, trans. Thomas Common, in *The Case of Wagner* (London, 1899); Henri Bergson, *Laughter*, trans. Cloudesley Brereton and Fred Rothwell (New York: Macmillan, 1911), Chap. III, Sect. 1; and Machen, *Hieroglyphics*, Chap. 1. Cf. Edgar Jepson, *Memories of an Edwardian and Neo-Georgian* (London: Richards, 1937), pp. 54-55: "The great things, great love, great music, great literature, great

Joyce and Virginia Woolf, for whom art is born of "some moment of passionate experience," "lightnings of intuition," unexpected visionary flashes, and for whom—for Yeats in particular—the aim of art is to induce exaltation, to seek out and convey an almost disembodied ecstasy.[35] What may seem a minor theme in the imaginative life of this period somehow in tentacular fashion reaches out and exemplifies the whole.

---

art do induce ecstasy; they set us outside ourselves, and in touch with reality. . . ."

[35] Cf. W. B. Yeats, "Anima Hominis," Sect. V (*Per Amica Silentia Lunae*): ". . . For the awakening, for the vision, for the revelation of reality, tradition offers us a . . . word—ecstasy."

CHAPTER 8

The Will to Believe: Emergent Existentialism

The third and final application of my thesis is at once the most amorphous and yet the most sustaining of them all in this period's journey through despair. The terms of this chapter's double title need close definition if the motif is to be brought clearly into focus. As Professor Houghton discusses the "will to believe" in the earlier decades of the nineteenth century, *belief* appears mainly to have one meaning; it is a conviction that some larger conception of life is taken as having firm validity, a fixed part of the real nature of things, so certain that one is willing to act upon it.[1] By the turn of the century at least two more elements need to be added to the meaning of belief. In William James's usage belief becomes largely an educated bet; since man can obviously not know everything of his earthly condition, and since he nevertheless must assume *something* as being true if he is to act at all, he must hold some belief *pro tempore*, all the while aware that later evidence may prove his belief to be ill-founded.[2] Within the period of our consideration the meaning of belief advances one stage further—to shun all absolutes, to view the true nature of things as being unknowable, and then, willfully

[1] See Walter E. Houghton, *Victorian Frame of Mind: 1830-1870* (New Haven: Yale University Press, 1957), Chap. 4.
[2] "The Will to Believe," in *The Will to Believe and Other Essays in Popular Philosophy* (London: Longmans, Green, 1903).

and knowingly, find or fabricate illusions and *believe* in them. This is the vein of Richard Jefferies' illusion of immortality—when "the spirit goes out like a flame, still I shall have had the glory of that thought." Or of W. H. Davies:

> Life has no joy
> Except we cherish some
> Illusive dream.

My usage of the term *belief* must be accepted in all of these modes: as acceptance that a conclusion is *true*; as a "working arrangement" by which we accept some creed *pro tempore*; and as an outright embracement of confessed illusion. "Order," Forster was to pronounce, "is something evolved from within, not something imposed from without."[3]

In such a spectrum of meanings the existential quality is readily apparent. The term *existentialism* is here used in a very general but I trust clearly definable sense. I do not insist on its technical and philosophical premise that "existence precedes essence" or that existentialism expresses the need to protest the depersonalization of the modern world. What impinged on the literary mind of the 1880-1914 period was a disposition which I think marks most existential thought, a resolve that, however bleak, hostile, or incomprehensible man's predicament is, nevertheless man must *be* and must *find significance in being*. That is what I mean by existentialism in this chapter, and

[3] Quotations from Jefferies, *Story of My Heart* (1883), Chap. 3 (the theme is also touched on recurrently in Chap. 4); Davies, "The Proven"; and E. M. Forster, "Art for Art's Sake" (1949), in Forster, *Two Cheers for Democracy* (New York: Harcourt, Brace, and World, 1951), p. 90.

I find it to be a growing resolve—to find and to *believe* in a significant existence for the human spirit in spite of all the seeming obstacles and refutations which confront us. It is a resolve to find an answer to Rilke's question, How is one to live in an incomprehensible world?

So far so good. But we still must pause to recognize that the will to believe and to affix a meaning to life, or to create a meaning within it, is by no means a phenomenon of these three decades alone. Generally speaking, one might argue that it would be difficult to find another century or another culture in which truths of fact and value and conduct were more urgently sought for than they were in this England of the late nineteenth century, but there have indeed been many times before and after these years when man has felt called upon to navigate without stars. King Lear comes to mind with his towering awareness of oblivion—"Never, never, never, never, never" —and yet faith is still there in his words to Cordelia: "Upon such sacrifices, my Cordelia,/ The gods themselves throw incense." (Shakespeare, as John Davidson remarked, "found the world an empty nut and put a kernel into it.") But within the nineteenth century, the moments of chartless despair appear to become more frequently manifest in the literary consciousness. There is the Romantic's "willing suspension of the disbelief,"[4] and the post-Romantic's willful seclusion in a world shut away from reality (Rossetti's mirrored room, Aubrey Beardsley's candlelit studio). In Clough the resolve is stronger to *impose* a significance and belief on the bleak intransigent world:

[4] Quotations from *King Lear*, V, iii; Davidson, "Tete-a-Tete, Parolles. Hamlet," *Speaker* (May 13, 1899), pp. 553-554; and Coleridge, *Biographia Literaria* (1817), Chap. 14.

Hope evermore and believe, O man, for e'en
    as thy thought
So are the things that thou see'st; e'en as
    thy hope and belief.
Cowardly art thou and timid? they rise to
    provoke thee against them;
Hast thou courage? enough, see them exult-
    ing to yield.
Yea, the rough rock, the dull earth, the wild
    sea's furying waters
(Violent say'st thou and hard, mighty thou
    think'st to destroy),
All with ineffable longing are waiting their
    Invader,
All with one varying voice, call to him,
    Come and subdue.[5]

In the new Catholicism the point was often made—most clearly in Wilfrid Ward's *The Wish to Believe* (1885)—that belief will rarely come to the apathetic heart, or by the passive submission of the mind to things. Belief must be longed for, struggled for, willed. "Even during the period when I practically believed nothing," wrote Chesterton, "I believed in what some have called 'the wish to believe.'" Said Unamuno, "Faith is in its essence simply a matter of will, not of reason; . . . to believe is to wish to believe, and to believe in God is, before all and above all, to wish that there may be a God." Much more recently, Joseph Wood Krutch has concluded that ". . . in a universe as badly adapted as this one to human as distinguished from animal needs this ability to will a belief may

[5] "Hope Evermore and Believe!" (1862).

bestow an enormous vital advantage. . . ."[6] Even in the activists there is an implied intrusion into an empty world of man's will to believe, and a search through action for the solace of commitment. "Action is consolatory," says Conrad. "Only in the conduct of our action can we find the sense of mastery over the Fates."[7]

The inner compulsion, then, to will a belief and to bring into the outer world a significance which was not there before is not new at the turn of the century. My purpose is to demonstrate that the motive became accelerated and intensified in this period, and I think there is abundant evidence to show that it was. The temptation is simply to cite the abundant and pervasive amount of evidence and let it speak for itself. There is Lionel Johnson's insistence that "the human mind, to preserve itself, must give life meaning, surrounding it with 'elaborate ritual,' " that indeed "life *is* ritual" (italics mine).[8] John Butler Yeats insists that "poetry concerns itself with the creation of Paradises. I use the word in the plural for there are as many paradises as there are individual men—nay—as many as there are separate feelings." This might seem well enough by itself as a random comment, but the motif is taken

[6] Quotations from G. K. Chesterton, *Autobiography* (London: Hutchinson, 1937), p. 165; Miguel de Unamuno, *Tragic Sense of Life*, trans. J. E. Crawford Flitch (New York: Dover, 1954), p. 114; and Krutch, *The Modern Temper* (New York: Harcourt, Brace, 1929), Sect. 4.

[7] Joseph Conrad, *Nostromo* (1903-1904), Chap. 6.

[8] The phrases are quoted from Johnson by W. B. Yeats. See Barbara Charlesworth, *Dark Passages: The Decadent Consciousness in Victorian Literature* (Madison: University of Wisconsin Press, 1965), p. 87; and Yeats, "The Tragic Generation," Bk. IV, Sect. 5, in *Trembling of the Veil*, in *The Autobiography of William Butler Yeats* (New York: Doubleday, 1958), p. 201.

time and again in this period by minds of entirely different cast. Arthur Ransome (interpreting Remy de Gourmont) wrote that "there are as many truths as brains." And Havelock Ellis reiterates: "We have to recognise that even the humblest of us is entitled to his own 'universe.'" The notion that man *can* make his own world was widespread on the continent. Schopenhauer is again the prophet on this theme: "The events of the world will have significance only so far as they are the letters out of which we may read the Idea of man, but not in and for themselves." It was so with Pater's Marius, "constructing the world for himself in great measure from within, by the exercise of meditative power." And it is thus that William Butler Yeats viewed the making of a poet: "In our time we are agreed that we 'make our own souls' out of some one of the great poets of ancient times, or out of Shelley or Wordsworth, or Goethe or Balzac, or Flaubert, or Count Tolstoy, . . . or out of Whistler's pictures. . . ."[9] So created, the poet moves on "to make and unmake reality" and to "make the truth."[10] "Call earth heaven," David-

[9] The quotations are from John B. Yeats, letter to W. B. Yeats, May 10, 1914, in *Letters to His Son W. B. Yeats and Others, 1869-1922* (London: Faber and Faber, 1944), p. 179. (Cf. Conrad, "Preface" to *The Nigger of the Narcissus* [1897]: "Fiction . . . must be . . . like all art, the appeal of one temperament to all other innumerable temperaments whose subtle and resistless power endows passing events with their true meaning . . . .") Ransome, "Remy de Gourmont," in *Portraits and Speculations* (London: Macmillan, 1913); Ellis, *Dance of Life* (London: Constable, 1923), p. 203n; Schopenhauer, *World As Will and Idea*, I, Bk. III, Sect. 35; Pater, *Marius*, Chap. 2; and W. B. Yeats, "William Blake and the Imagination" (1897), in *Essays and Introductions* (New York: Macmillan, 1961).

[10] See Richard Ellmann, *Yeats: The Man and the Masks* (New York: Dutton, 1958), pp. 187, 287.

son's Cosmo Mortimer attests, "and you would have heaven."[11]

Two manifestations in particular of the will to believe deserve our attention, apart from such scattered and diffuse evidence as we have seen thus far. One, already briefly encountered before, is the widespread notion that it is the task of man to create God. Voltaire had remarked long before that if there were no God it would be necessary to invent him. Now the time had come when for Nietzsche, as for many of his contemporaries, God was dead; the human imagination must turn to the task of re-creating Him. Again there are premonitions in the literature before; Carlyle maintained that ". . . the belief in heaven is derived from the nobility of man." The theme persists after the strict chronological limit of our period, in Unamuno's "we have created God in order to save the Universe from nothingness. . . ." As the headnote to a section of his *Interpretations of Poetry and Religion* (1900), George Santayana quotes Jean Lahor: "Man has henceforth this cause of pride: that he has bethought himself of justice in a universe without justice, and has put justice there." Pater's Marius is also impelled (Chap. 2) to construct "the world for himself in great measure from within." Closer to our own time we have Jennet Jourdemayne's cry:

> . . . If all is a pretty fiction
> To distract the cherubim and seraphim
> Who so continually do cry, the least
> I can do is to fill the curled shell of the world
> With human deep-sea sound, and hold it to

[11] John Davidson, *Perfervid* (London, 1890), p. 117.

The ear of God, until he has appetite
To taste our salt sorrow on his lips.[12]

But I believe that it is within the imaginative climate of the 1880-1914 period that the necessity of man's creating God first becomes clearly and widely manifest. One finds it in Havelock Ellis: "It is only when we place God at the End, not at the Beginning, that the Universe falls into order. God is an Unutterable Sigh in the Human Heart. . . ." And in Bergson, who writes that man's responsibility is to fulfill ". . . the essential function of the universe, which is a machine for the making of gods." The idea is apparent most of all in George Bernard Shaw, for whom the urge to create a God for mankind, an evolving heaven on earth, became a major impetus to his life and writing. Granted, Shaw's view found only a part of its motive in an existentialist resolve to believe, and most of its motive came from a metaphysic of evolution and the Life Force which made it possible for him, by putting God into the distant future, to bring a perfect God into harmony with a manifestly imperfect world. But still and necessarily the insistent will to believe is there in the Shavian gospel. "The Life Force is God in the act of creating Himself; and we, as His instruments and helpers, can take heart and courage from this great opportunity and responsibility." Such was the crux of Shaw's exchange with Tolstoi: "To me God does not yet exist; but there is a creative force constantly struggling to evolve an executive organ of godlike knowledge and power: that is, to achieve om-

[12] Quotations from Carlyle, quoted in John Tyndall, "Science and Man" (1877), in *Fragments of Science* (6th edn.; 2 vols.; London, 1879), II, 372; Unamuno, *Tragic Sense of Life*, p. 154; and Christopher Fry, *The Lady's Not for Burning*, Act III.

nipotence and omniscience; and every man and woman born is a fresh attempt to achieve this object."[13] Presumably all socialists of this period longed and worked for a more equitable, harmonious fellowship of man on earth. But with Shaw the longing gained added strength and dimension from his views of evolution and from his will to believe in the emergent reality of a better world.

The second important manifestation of the will to believe in this period is the gathering conviction that, since order had failed man in the external world, he had to fall back on the construction of an internal order in the world. The motive is in close accord with the accelerated move toward subjectivism in the imagination of the age generally and its increasingly poignant sense of loneliness and isolation, with "each mind," in Pater's words, "keeping as a solitary prisoner its own dream of a world." The necessity of willfully constructing an order of one's own to live by and to impose on the surrounding chaos became overt in many authors of this generation. For some it simply took the form of an insistence that the will is stronger than the reason, and that all things are "plastic to our will." Even H. G. Wells would say, "Will is stronger than Fact, it can mould and overcome Fact"; and Osman Edward quotes Verhaeren as significantly insisting that "the fact and the world serve simply . . . as phenomena, condemned to perpetual variation, and . . . , in fine,

[13] The quotations are from Ellis, *Impressions and Comments* (London: Constable, 1920), p. 190, entry for August 18, 1913; Bergson, concluding sentence of *The Two Sources of Morality and Religion*, trans. R. Ashley Audra and Cloudesley Brereton (New York: Meridian, 1935); Archibald Henderson, *George Bernard Shaw: Man of the Century* (New York: Appleton-Century-Crofts, 1956), p. 581; and Shaw, letter to Tolstoi, February 14, 1910, quoted in *ibid.*, p. 589.

merely the figments of our brain. It is the idea which de-
termines them by adaptation or evocation." With Yeats
the belief that "the eye altering alters all" became central
—as it had been with Blake—and from this conviction
came his magnificent resolve as a poet. It is up from man's
emotional nature, bestial though that may be, that all lad-
ders start, from ". . . the foul rag-and-bone shop of the
heart."[14] "I doubt indeed," wrote Yeats, "if the crude circumstance of the world, which seems to create all our
emotions, does more than reflect as in multiplying mirrors,
the emotions that have come to solitary men in moments
of poetical contemplation." And again:

> Our towns are copied fragments from our breast;
> And all man's Babylons strive but to impart
> The grandeurs of his Babylonian heart.[15]

But there is another author for whom the imposing of
a firm subjective order on life was a commanding motif of
the imagination—Joseph Conrad. Indeed I submit that the
theme of this study, its sources and applications, *can* add
significantly to the critical understanding of Conrad's
work. I do not offer to contradict studies which treat Conrad as philosopher or as moralist, nor critics who have
read him primarily as an artist of the Impressionist school,
whose leading motives were aesthetic. E. M. Forster con-

[14] Quotations are from Pater, "Conclusion," *Renaissance*; Jefferies, *Stories of My Heart*, Chap. 9; Wells, *A Modern Utopia* (London, 1905), Chap. 11, Sect. 5; Edwards, "Emile Verhaeren," *Savoy*,
No. 7 (November 1896), p. 70; Blake, "The Mental Traveller"
(ca. 1803); and William Butler Yeats, "The Circus Animals'
Desertion" (1939).

[15] Both quotations are from Yeats, "The Symbolism of Poetry"
(1900), Sect. 2, in *Essays and Introductions*.

cludes, I think wrongly, that Conrad had "no creed, in fact. Only opinions. . . . Opinions held under the semblance of eternity, girt with the sea, crowned with the stars, and therefore easily mistaken for a creed." Conrad himself may seem to concur, as when he writes in his "Author's Note" to *Nostromo*: "My reasons were not moral, but artistic." But it was also Conrad who wrote: "In truth every novelist must begin by creating for himself a world, great or little, in which he can honestly believe." Yeats might well have given support to such a view: "When the external world is no more the standard of reality, we will learn again that the great passions are angels of God." If this is "no creed, in fact," it would be difficult to find a right name for it.[16]

Conrad elsewhere wrote of "some such truth or some such illusion—I don't care how you call it, there is so little difference, and the difference means so little."[17] It should be apparent that Conrad deeply shared in the disillusionment of this generation, and that his major imaginative response in combatting it lay in a willful construction of an internal sense of order and light, which he then sought to impose upon the external darkness. To see this point more clearly is not to resolve or to dissipate the many ambiguities in Conrad's work, but rather to make those

[16] Quotations from Forster, "Joseph Conrad: A Note," in *Abinger Harvest* (New York: Harcourt, Brace, and World, 1936), p. 138; Conrad, "Author's Note" to *Nostromo* and "Books" (1905), in Walter F. Wright, ed., *Joseph Conrad on Fiction* (Lincoln: University of Nebraska Press, 1964), p. 79; and Yeats, "The Body of the Father Christian Rosencrux" (1895), in *Essays and Introductions*, p. 197.

[17] *Lord Jim* (1900), Chap. 21.

ambiguities more visible, acute, and poignant—and to make the greatness of his achievement more apparent.[18]

Consider the plight of man as it is seen recurrently in Conrad's work. Around him is darkness, a sea of storms and trouble, a "cruel futility." We do not know what has made it so—whether "implacable destiny," "Dark Powers," or some "fatal imperfection of all the gifts of life." What we do know is that we are here "only on sufferance" in this "formidable Work of the Seven Days, into which mankind seems to have blundered unbidden."[19]

What then may man do, according to Conrad? Be *aware* of his predicament and sensitive to it, first of all, for "those who do not feel do not count." Have courage enough, second, "to face the darkness," and " 'to the destructive element submit yourself. . . .' " That is the only advice Captain McWhirr can give to Jukes in the gale: " 'Keep her facing it. They may say what they like, but the heaviest seas run with the wind. Facing it—always facing it—that's the way to get through. You are a young sailor. Face it. That's enough for any man. Keep a cool head.' "[20] And then for each man there is the tempera-

[18] The same general imaginative response is found in Virginia Woolf; see Joan Bennett, *Virginia Woolf: Her Art as a Novelist* (2nd edn.; Cambridge, Eng.: Cambridge University Press, 1964), p. 12. Cf. Geoffrey Bruun, *Nineteenth Century European Civilization, 1815-1914* (New York: Oxford, 1960), p. 149, where he speaks of the "rediscovery that the artist was himself the most important element in his art, and that the thinker not only perceived but also imposed form on the objective world . . . ."

[19] The phrases are from *Nostromo* (1904), Chap. 20, third paragraph; *Lord Jim* (1900), Chap. 34, fourth paragraph; *ibid.*, Chap. 10; *Victory* (1914), Pt. III, Chap. 4; *Lord Jim*, Chap. 5, second paragraph; and "The Shadow-Line" (1915), Chap. 5.

[20] Quotations from *Lord Jim*, Chap. 21; "Heart of Darkness" (1898), Pt. I; *Lord Jim*, Chap. 20; and *Typhoon*, Chap. 5.

ment, those "secret purposes" of the heart which give to his life the direction in which order may be found. It may be simply the "blinding hot glow of passionate purpose" of Lena in *Victory*, or Charles Gould's vague faith that "a man must work to some end." It may be merely "efficiency" which saves us, or the single-minded application of some one talent, "an honest concern for the right way of going to work," as in Towson's (or Towser's?) book on seamanship in "Heart of Darkness." Often it is an inner quality of "steadfastness," a "blessed stiffness" or "moral . . . posture," the sort of fidelity (so woefully to be betrayed) that marks the character of Nostromo. In the more difficult and complex novels, the harmony and coherence man seeks to impose on life takes on social and political dimensions and becomes that "sheltering conception of light and order which is our refuge" (Lord Jim's Patusan) or the "rallying point" in *Nostromo* of the San Tomé mine "for everything in the province that needed order and stability to live."[21] It is in one's twofold awareness of his predicament in life and of his "secret purposes" of the heart, and in the courage to face both awarenesses forthrightly, that one discovers his coherence and his "truth" in life. That is why the protagonist of "The Shadow-Line" must "inexplicably" surrender his days and cushy berth on the Eastern ship: "I felt—how shall I express it?—that there was no truth to be got out of them." In the struggle, perhaps futile, against the powers of dark-

---

[21] The phrases are all from Conrad: "Author's Note" to *Nostromo*; *Victory*, Chap. 9; *Nostromo*, Chap. 6; "Heart of Darkness," Pt. I; *ibid.*, Pt. II; *Lord Jim*, Chap. 10; *ibid.*, Chap. 5; *ibid.*; *Lord Jim*, Chap. 33; and *Nostromo*, Chap. 8. The quality of stoic steadfastness creates characters in Conrad similar to Hardy's Diggory Venn and Gabriel Oak.

ness, one must keep faith and remain true to that dream which is born into the heart of every man who feels. In the end man is seen, as we last see Lord Jim, as "only a speck, a tiny white speck, . . . catching all the dim light left upon a sombre coast and the darkened sea. . . ."[22]

To repeat, my point is that there is a strong inclination in all of Conrad to view the source of human belief as being not external and learned, but internal and willed. The meaningful order of life is made of man's will and imagination, not of some higher harmony in the world in which he lives, or in the environment of his life or beyond it. There is a beautiful moment in *Nostromo* in which Conrad speaks of the desire in man's life "to leave a correct impression of the feelings, like a light by which the action may be seen when personality is gone, gone where no light of investigation can ever reach the truth which every death takes out of the world."[23] The truth abides in man, not in the world around him. To see this is to understand more clearly Marlow's view, which otherwise might seem perverse or cryptic: "To him the meaning of an episode was not inside like a kernel but outside, enveloping the tale which brought it out only as a glow brings out a haze, in the likeness of one of these misty halos that sometimes are made visible by the spectral illumination of moonshine."[24]

It is fitting to conclude this book with this motif of man's will to believe and with his gathering resolve in these years to find the meaning of existence in existence itself. It is a theme which springs directly from the imagi-

[22] Quotations from "The Shadow-Line," Chap. 1; *Lord Jim*, Chap. 35; and *ibid.*, Chap. 43.

[23] *Nostromo*, Chap. 15.   [24] "Heart of Darkness," Pt. I.

native crisis of the time—the loss of faith in the transcendent, revulsion against the kind of world being revealed by the reason, and a deepening skepticism about man's ability to establish any coherent relationship between himself and the world of "fact." At the same time, this theme does bespeak synthesis; it brings into kinship many authors, works, and moods which before have seemed quite unrelated. Most of all, the will to believe elicited the discovery, by the reformulation of the terms of man's imaginative life, which was to be, in my opinion, the most consoling, rewarding, and resolving of any that emerged from these baffled years—and which led Yeats, for example, to "rejoice in the midst of tragedy,"[25] and enabled man's imagination to achieve its journey through despair.

From the strengthening will to believe it is a short step to the splendid paradox in which the deepest despair becomes the source of greatest achievement. Dostoevsky's underground man discovered that "in despair occur the most intense enjoyments, especially when one is very acutely conscious of one's hopeless position." Unamuno was to propose "that many of the greatest heroes, perhaps the greatest of all, have been men of despair and . . . by despair they have accomplished their mighty works."[26] Yeats saw that "the poet finds and makes his mask in disappointment, the hero in defeat"; and Chesterton knew

[25] Letter to Dorothy Wellesley, July 26, 1935, in William Butler Yeats, *Letters*, ed. Allen Wade (New York: Macmillan, 1954), p. 838.
[26] Quotations from Fyodor Dostoevsky, *Notes from Underground and The Grand Inquisitor*, trans. Ralph E. Matlaw (New York: Dutton, 1960), Pt. I, Sect. 2; and Unamuno, *Tragic Sense of Life*, Chap. 6.

that "the more hopeless . . . the situation the more hopeful must be the man." It is the cry of the Saxon chieftain to his troops:

Hige sceal Þē heardra, heorte Þē cēnre,
mōd sceal Þē māre, Þē ūre maegen lȳtlaỗ.

[Soul shall grow harder, heart the keener,
Spirit the greater, as our might grows less.][27]

With the passing of a great and long tradition of faith, man's fate had come full circle. After centuries of assurance, or glimpses, or intimations of a bond with some higher harmony, man is once more alone against a world either hostile or incomprehensible, or perhaps simply without meaning. And it is just at the end of the nineteenth century and the beginning of the twentieth, as shown in the literature of the period, that man gradually and "emergently" finds the courage to be and to believe, to discover within himself the ennobling mask and the order which had deserted him. He stands forth again, ridiculous but unconquered, aware that within his mind and imagination lies some semblance of the resource which he thought had been banished from this world. He is learning, as did Richard Jefferies, that he can, after all, "leave his gods, and lift up his ideal beyond them." Or, like G. K. Chesterton, he is finding that the human mind

[27] Quotations from W. B. Yeats, "Anima Hominis," Sect. 9, *Per Amica Silentia Lunae* (New York: Macmillan, 1918); G. K. Chesterton, *Heretics* (London: John Lane, 1914), Chap. 9; and "The Battle of Maldon," ll. 311-312 (trans. mine). The poignancy of the "Maldon" lines suggests an explanation of our contemporary renewed affinity with works like the *Beowulf*, and the striking similarities between the vital code of Ernest Hemingway, for example, and the Anglo-Saxon.

is infinitely transmuting; everything that has passed through it "has become a thing incurably mysterious and infinite; this mortal has put on immortality."[28] But the clearest voice is again that of Joseph Conrad: "The human heart is vast enough to contain all the world. It is valiant enough to bear the burden. . . ."[29]

[28] Quotations from Jefferies' essay of May 1886, quoted in Henry S. Salt, *The Faith of Richard Jefferies* (London, 1906), p. 5; and Chesterton, *Heretics*, Chap. 11.

[29] *Lord Jim*, Chap. 34.

Afterword on Bibliography

There is a pattern in the affairs of the bibliography of an age. Autobiographies come first, chronologically, with their special virtues of immediacy and directness of vision, and their limitations in the partiality of that vision or in its prejudice and myopic disproportion. The first general studies and attempts to assess the period then follow, though often interwoven with reminiscences or marked by a tendency to dwell on the dramatically visible and the historically apparent. For the period between 1880 and 1914, a special disproportion is lent to such studies, owing to the apocalyptic impact of the First World War, post-War Stracheyism, and a woefully widespread assumption that in *fin-de-siècle* literature all that glisters must be yellow. Then come the more thorough and scholarly studies of individual authors, based on previously unknown or inaccessible manuscript resources, followed by publication of the resources themselves—letters, diaries, notebooks —until at last critical attitudes develop whose depth and width of perspective permit a balanced assessment of the special character of the literary culture of an age, the sources from which it sprang, and the stages and trends to which it led.

It seems a perversity of *homo sapiens* that he must proceed so, never substantially knowing the significance of his present until it has slipped at least several decades into the past. But this was true of the Metaphysicals, of Alexander Pope, of the Romantics, and of the great Victorians. And of the writers of the generation between 1880 and 1914 the same is true; the time for their fullest and most balanced assessment is just arriving.

The literary autobiographies of writers of this period are legion. Those of Yeats (1914, 1920), Mallock (1920), Douglas (1929), Rhys (1931), Rothenstein (1931, 1932), Wells (1934), Chesterton (1936), Ellis (1940), Leonard Woolf (1960 and following), and Compton Mackenzie (1963 and following) are only a few of the most revealing autobiographies recalling the period. One doubts if there has ever been another age of English literature whose participants were so urgently prompted to call it back to memory in later life, and to tell "how it was."

Early general studies of the time include W. G. Blaikie Murdoch's *Renaissance of the Nineties* (1911), Bernard Muddiman's *Men of the Nineties* (1920), Osbert Burdett's *Beardsley Period* (1925), E. F. Benson's *As We Were* (1930), and John Lewis May's *John Lane and the Nineties* (1936). Of this kind the best are Holbrook Jackson's *Eighteen-Nineties* (1913), in which the journalist's broad sweep of the period gives a valuable overall view, and Richard Le Gallienne's *Romantic '90s* (1926), in which the perspectives of time and geographic distance have revealed an Olympian vision rare in the reminiscential studies of this age. I have been told by one who was very much a part of the literary scene at the *fin de siècle* that these seven volumes, plus Vincent O'Sullivan's *Opinions* (1959), constitute "all you need to know" to understand that flamboyant age; "you've got them all!" In Katherine Lyon Mix's *Study in Yellow* (1960) these studies have been given a compendious summary. One could almost be convinced that these works about England at the turn of the century are the last word on the subject, yet it must be apparent that, valuable as these studies are, the field has been artificially limited in them. They focus the reader's attention again and again on the same pivotal episodes: Ernest Dowson's fashion of love, Whistler's repartee to Oscar Wilde, Lionel Johnson's fractured skull, Francis Thompson's hopeless and anonymous posting of his poems from general delivery, Charing Cross Post Office. In every account the trials and collapse of Wilde are detailed as the death-knell of a sick generation.

In the 1930s and the 1940s, more comprehensive attempts were made to sketch the pattern of the period. Esmé Wingfield-Stratford's trilogy, *Victorian Tragedy* (1930), *Victorian Sunset* (1932), and *Victorian Aftermath* (1934), sought the unifying elements in social history and the consequent tides of taste. H. V. Routh's *Towards the Twentieth Century* (1937) and *English Literature and Ideas in the Twentieth Century* (1946) are valuable studies in the vein of intellectual and spiritual history; William Gaunt's *Pre-Raphaelite Tragedy* (1942), *Aesthetic Adventure* (1945), and *March of the Moderns* (1949) are valuable chronicles of the aesthetic experience of the time. Although the element of historical and biographical record looms large in these series, they provide useful groundwork and bring much relevant information into orderly sequence. Essays in interpretation also appeared in the 1930s, such as Granville Hicks's *Figures in Transition* (1939), which sees the transition as something fundamentally socioeconomic, and Malcolm Elwin's astounding (considering its date) *Old Gods Falling* (1939). Elwin takes the presiding animus of the turn of the century to be a righteously indignant revolt against the idols of Victorianism, and gives 1918 (!) as the moment of triumph —when "household gods of Respectability, Prudery, and Humbug" were overthrown. One can only agree with

Albert Guérard that, in the 1930s at least, this period was "not yet capable of dispassionate historical treatment; we are only beginning to discern, in the whirling turbid flood, the main stream from the eddies."[1]

Since the Second World War biographies and critical studies about the writers of the period have appeared with increasing frequency: Lang (1946), Wilde (1947, 1948, 1963), Bennett (1953, 1963), Beerbohm (1960, 1965), Besant (1960, 1964), Le Gallienne (1960), Mivart (1960), Stevenson (1960), Davidson (1961), George Russell (1961, 1962), Pater (1962), Wells (1962), Rupert Brooke (1963), Davies (1963), Gissing (1963), Machen (1963), Jefferies (1964), Symonds (1964), Zangwill (1964)—the list is symptomatic, and by no means complete.[2] Studies

[1] Quotations from Elwin, p. 41; and Albert Guérard, *Art for Art's Sake* (New York: Lothrop, Lee and Shepard, 1936), pp. 81-82.

[2] Repeating that this list is incomplete and merely suggestive, the titles I have in mind in this paragraph are:

1946: Roger L. Green, *Andrew Lang* (Leicester, Eng.: Ward).

1947: Edouard Roditi, *Oscar Wilde* (Norfolk, Conn.: New Directions).

1948: H. Montgomery Hyde, ed., *The Trials of Oscar Wilde:* (London: William Hodge).

1953: Reginald Pound, *Arnold Bennett* (New York: Harcourt, Brace).

1960: S. N. Behrman, *Portrait of Max* (New York: Random House). Arthur H. Nethercot, *The First Five Lives of Annie Besant* (Chicago: University of Chicago Press). Richard Whittington-Egan and Geoffrey Smerdon, *The Quest of the Golden Boy: The Life and Letters of Richard Le Gallienne* (London: Unicorn). Joseph W. Gruber, *A Conscience in Conflict; The Life of St. George Jackson Mivart* (New York: Columbia University Press). Elsie N. Caldwell, *Last Witness for Robert Louis Stevenson* (Norman: University of Oklahoma Press).

1961: J. Benjamin Townsend, *John Davidson* (New Haven:

of Conan Doyle, Hardy, and Rudyard Kipling appear
with frequency. In biography and criticism of Conrad,
Ford, Lawrence, Shaw, and Yeats, there is no end to the
making of books. Such studies attest to the growing awareness that our understanding of the culture of this transitional period is of significance, and crucial to an understanding of our own; and they add measurably to our
ability to achieve that understanding.

Next come the letters, abundantly. One must admire
scholars like Professor Dan H. Laurence, in his editing
of the Shaw correspondence (1965, plus three volumes to
come!)—Herculean labor, yet immensely productive, and
illuminating to our search for a balanced, "final" estimate

Yale University Press). Alan Denson, *The Printed Writings of George W. Russell (AE): A Bibliography* (Evans-
ton: Northwestern University Press).

1962: Alan Denson, ed., *Letters by A.E.* (London: Abelard-
Schuman). Germain d'Hangest, *Walter Pater: L'Homme
et L'Oeuvre* (2 vols., Paris: Didier). Gernard Bergonzi,
Early H. G. Wells (Toronto: University of Toronto
Press).

1963: H. Montgomery Hyde, *Oscar Wilde: The Aftermath*
(New York: Farrar, Straus). James G. Hepburn, *The
Art of Arnold Bennett* (Bloomington: Indiana University
Press). Richard J. Stonesifer, *W. H. Davies* (London:
Jonathan Cape). Jacob Korg, *George Gissing* (Seattle:
University of Washington Press). Aldan Reynolds, *Ar-
thur Machen* (London: Richard).

1964: Christopher Hassall, *Rupert Brooke* (London: Faber &
Faber). Arthur H. Nethercot, *The Last Four Lives of
Annie Besant* (Chicago: University of Chicago Press).
Samuel J. Looker and Crichton Porteous, *Richard Jefferies* (London: Baker). Phyllis Grosskurth, *John Addington Symonds* (London: Longmans). Maurice Wohl-
gelernter, *Israel Zangwill* (New York: Columbia University Press).

1965: David Cecil, *Max* (Boston: Houghton Mifflin).

of the mercurial G.B.S. Similar, if lesser, reevaluations must be effected by the recent publication of the letters of Beerbohm, Butler, Ford, Gissing, Kipling, Lawrence, Lear, Russell, and Wilde. Letters give a peculiarly penetrating *venue* to an author's work—immediacy, uninhibited responses, precision in chronology, clues to mood and temper. Rupert Hart-Davis's brilliant edition of Wilde's correspondence, for example, has given us an Oscar who can never again relapse into the poseur and the charlatan, the object lesson in moral degradation for which he has often mistakenly been taken. Perhaps the most valuable single addition of all to our knowledge of this period has come and continues to come in the pages of the journal *English Literature in Transition*.

Thus the materials for an accurate and discriminating view of the culture of the 1880-1914 period are gradually becoming available. Edmund Wilson's *Axel's Castle* (1931) was an extraordinarily prescient study of the time, and retains its value. It concentrates on one major aspect of the period, the rise of symbolism. Morse Peckham's *Beyond the Tragic Vision* (1962) and Stanley Edgar Hyman's *The Tangled Bank* (1962) are far-ranging and provocative overviews both of these years and of their larger context. More limited and directed interpretations of the age have been inclined to consider its culture mainly as the seedbed and preparation for our own. H. V. Routh's *Towards the Twentieth Century* (1937) by its very title denotes this special line of consideration, as do William York Tindall's *Forces in Modern British Literature* (1956) and Ellmann and Feidelson's *The Modern Tradition* (1965). Frank Kermode's *Romantic Image* (1957) does more to study and assess the emergent cultural values of the time in and for themselves. Barbara Charlesworth's *Dark Passages* (1965), for all its moral prejudgments, is very much the sort of study that is needed now.

It will be difficult and it will take time to describe and evaluate the cultural character and achievement of this age. This book has sought to take a first step in that direction.

Index

Campbell, R. J., 10, 59, 76, 78
Capes, Bernard, 16
Carlyle, Thomas, xiii, 3, 8, 9, 23, 24, 66, 91, 105-106, 117, 142, 183-84
Carpenter, Edward, 31, 51, 64, 70, 71, 73, 74, 78, 85, 95, 99, 131, 162-63, 169-70
Carroll, Lewis [Charles Lutwidge Dodgson], 61
Cary, Joyce, 96-97
chance, 45-47
Charlesworth, Barbara, 19, 20, 36, 122, 130, 133, 145, 172, 181
Chaucer, Geoffrey, 101
Chesterton, G. K., xiii, xviii, 9, 10, 16, 17, 44, 67, 93, 122, 180-81, 191-92, 193
childhood, 60-61
Chittick, V.L.O., 128
Clifford, William Kingdon, 78
Clodd, Edward, 93
closed field, 34-36, 185
Clough, Arthur Hugh, 66, 179
Cobden-Sanderson, T. J., 167
Coleridge, Samuel T., 68, 102, 110, 133, 168, 179
consciousness, 83; as disease, 59-60, 64, 65, 76; cosmic, 85, 169: See also subconsciousness, unconsciousness
comedy, 97
Common, Thomas, 98, 175
Comte, Augusta, 97
Conrad, Joseph, xiv, xv, 9, 30, 32, 50, 63, 89, 90, 100, 109, 139, 181, 182, 186-93
consistency, 87
Cornwell, Ethel F., 168
Corvo, Baron, 8

Crabbe, George, 158
Crackenthorpe, Hubert, 15, 111
Cramb, J. A., 10

Dallas, E. S., 87, 104, 106
dance, 127-29, 168, 170
dandyism, 141
Darrow, Clarence, 48
Darwin, Charles, xiv, xxii, 22, 23, 34, 37-48, 66, 75, 76, 81, 83, 84, 85, 86, 90, 161
Darwin, Francis, 39
Darwinian Theory, 37-48, 81, 85
Davidson, Donald, 12
Davidson, John, 9, 10, 32, 51, 52, 55, 56, 59-60, 66, 68-69, 77, 78, 86, 89, 90, 105, 130, 131, 132-33, 137, 164, 182-83, 179
Davies, W. H., 178
Dawe, W. Carlton, 112
decadence, 11-12
Dell, Floyd, 23
DeQuincey, Thomas, 158
determinism, xxii, 22-24, 26-30, 41, 43, 46, 48, 49, 58, 64, 109
Dewey, John, 47
Dickens, Charles, 3, 65, 91
Disraeli, Benjamin, 39, 141
Donne, John, 6, 154
Dostoevsky, Fyodor, 27, 59-60, 91, 137, 149, 191
double, role of the, 137-40, 149
Doughty, Oswald, 36
Dowson, Ernest, xv, 11, 14, 24, 32, 104
Drummond, Henry, 6, 23
DuGard, Roger Martin, 24

earth, 73-77
Eddy, Mary Baker, 51

INDEX

Rossetti, Dante Gabriel, 36, 172, 179

Rothwell, Fred, 175

Routh, H. V., 30, 50

Ruskin, John, xvii, 73, 108, 111, 133

Russell, George [A.E.], 75

Ryals, Clyde de L., 12

Salinger, J. M., 61

Salt, Henry, 48, 73, 74, 77, 79, 96, 193

Salvation Army, 51

Sanday, W., 44

Santayana, George, 34, 114, 145, 183

Sartre, Jean-Paul, xii, 32, 135

Schopenhauer, Arthur, 57, 62-65, 76, 90, 91, 99, 104, 105, 107, 110, 136-37, 161, 182

Schreiner, Olive, 11, 148

Schweitzer, Albert, 13

scientific method, 25-27, 29, 38-39

Scott, Samuel Mathewson, 72, 112

self-development, 10, 66-67, 69-70, 105, 146

Selincourt, Ernest de, 157

Seward, Barbara, 117, 119

sex, 64-65

Shaftesbury, Anthony A. C., 68

Sharp, Cecil, 127

Sharp, Evelyn, 7, 128

Sharp, William, 137

Shaw, George Bernard, 5, 43, 64, 69-70, 77, 79, 80, 82, 83, 84, 85, 93, 95, 96, 97, 98, 184-85

Sheldon, Henry C., 27, 77

Shelley, Mary, 138

Shelley, Percy Bysshe, 77, 88, 105, 132, 156, 182

Shiel, M. P., 17, 106, 115, 137

Sickert, Walter, 141

Simpson, George Gaylord, 43

Sitwell, Edith, 50, 66

Smart, Christopher, 154

socialism, 9, 78, 79, 184-85

Socrates, 130

Spencer, Herbert, 42

Spencer, Theodore, 106, 166

Stephen, Leslie, 40, 56, 129

Stevenson, Robert Louis, 8, 9, 61, 112, 138, 140

Stirner, Max, 10, 68, 71

Strauss, David, 22

subconsciousness, 105, 169, 171

suicide, xxii, 17, 28, 45

Sullivan, Arthur, 167

Swinburne, Algernon Charles, xiv, xv, 11, 172

symbolism, 116-22, 142-43

Symonds, John, 94

Symonds, John Addington, 109

Symons, A. J. A., 8, 130

Symons, Arthur, xvii, 12, 55, 104, 106, 112, 114, 127, 141, 144, 145, 170-71, 172

Syrett, Netta, 92-93

Tennyson, Alfred Lord, 8, 9, 12, 36, 65, 91, 118, 136

Thackeray, W. M., 138

theosophy, 93-95

Thomas, Edward, 73, 75, 94, 131, 164

Thomas, Helen, 78

Thompson, Francis, 158, 160, 174-75

Thomson, James (B.V.), 31, 32

Thoreau, Henry David, 74, 96